The Mental Art
of Putting

The Mental Art of Putting

Using Your Mind to Putt Your Best: The Psychology of Great Putting

Patrick J. Cohn, Ph.D. and Robert K. Winters, Ph.D.

Taylor Trade Publishing
Lanham • New York • Oxford

Published by Taylor Trade Publishing
An imprint of The Rowman & Littlefield Publishing Group, Inc.
4501 Forbes Boulevard, Suite 200
Lanham, Maryland 20706

Distributed by National Book Network

The hardcover edition of this title was previously cataloged by the Library of Congress as follows:

Cohn, Patrick J., 1960–
        The mental art of putting : using your mind to putt your best / Patrick J. Cohn and Robert K. Winters
        p. cm.
        Includes bibliographical references (p.).
        1. Golf (Putting)—Psychological aspects. I. Winters, Robert K., 1953–   II. Title.
GV979.P8C64 1995
796.352'35—dc20   95-22030
                                                                                            CIP

ISBN 0-87833-282-0 (pbk. : alk. paper)

♾™ The paper used in this publication meets the minimum requirements of American National Standard for Information Sciences—Permanence of Paper for Printed Library Materials, ANSI/NISO Z39.48–1992.
Manufactured in the United States of America.

This book is dedicated to my mother Patricia Cohn, sisters Audrey and Lisa, and brother Paul, who stood beside me in times of adversity. I regret that my brother R. Martin Cohn and father Ralph D. Cohn cannot be with us to share our hardships and sorrows, and successes and joys.

Patrick J. Cohn, Ph.D.

I dedicate this book to my father, Dale Winters, and to the memory of my mother Ann, who helped me realize that I have special gifts to offer the world. I also dedicate this book to my brother Bill and sister Betsy, for their continued support, and to my wife April, and sons Jared and Blake for their unyielding love and support.

Robert K. Winters, Ph.D.

Contents

Foreword

P utting is considered a game in itself. It can be the most enjoyable or the most miserable part of the game. No matter how hard we strive to shoot a good score, if the putts don't go in when expected, we experience feelings of self-doubt and frustration. We wonder why the putts are not falling and say, "Why should I bother to hit good shots close, if I can't make the putts?" From beginners to players such as myself who have made a living playing golf, nothing is more devastating or expensive than missing that easy birdie putt or "gimme."

The harder we try in golf, the worse our results become. We practice longer and harder, try new putters, listen to the pros and teachers, and read putting technique books. With all our seemingly positive efforts, we do no better than before. Our efforts soon become efforts of desperation and searching for "the answer." We wonder where we went wrong—or did we? Maybe we need to look at ourselves and realign our thoughts and concepts of putting to get the results we want. This book was written with this goal in mind.

Robert Winters and Patrick Cohn realized this and have spent several years working with and studying players of all levels from beginners to top amateurs and professionals. Their culmination of years of working with players and studying golf has today given us the book, *The Mental Art of Putting*. Bob and Patrick have provided the golfing world with a unique, simple and fascinating book. The information they present in the book far surpasses that of any theoretical or mechanical golf books on the market today. The information is clear and makes sense.

During my playing years, I was privileged to have worked with Dave Pelz, author of *Putt Like the Pros*. Dave has been a friend and confidant to me in my years of frustration with putting. Dave rated me as one of the best ball strikers to have ever played the PGA Tour, however he has died with me on the greens. I now realize the overemphasis we placed on results, as well as technique, rather than focusing on the psychology and visual imagery needed to make putts.

I have known Bob Winters for over 20 years. As a tour player, I met many people with "new" ideas or a placebo for our problems. Tour pros are typically skeptical about "outsiders," but Bob helped me get past that because he had a different approach. I have had the pleasure of working with Bob on occasion since our first meeting in the mid '70s. Each time we worked together, I saw a more informed and concerned person. He taught me some great information about putting and golf, and I sensed he truly cared. Today, with his friend and co-author, Dr. Patrick Cohn, who wrote *The Mental Game of Golf*, they together have given us a practical, no-nonsense method to help us get the most out of putting.

The Mental Art of Putting has changed my attitude about putting. I have progressed from a mechanical and technique-oriented putter to one that uses psychology and visual factors that allow me to putt my best. This book has also changed my personal life. My life and business attitude are now focused on an attitude of success and the process of learning and understanding, rather than on an attitude of failure and inadequate results. *The Mental Art of Putting* will help change your putting attitude and help you choose how to think better. By changing your attitude, you can enjoy a more rewarding game.

Allen Miller
Veteran PGA Tour member and PGA Tour winner

Preface

Many people in golf call putting a game within a game. Others call it a black art, a mystic science, or an exercise in human patience. Great putting combines science, physics, psychology, luck, and human genius. By its very nature, putting stirs the emotions of anyone who plays or teaches golf. Golfers are biased one way or the other about putting: they either love it or they hate it. There is little ground in between. Years ago it was said that the legendary Ben Hogan felt putting was not golf, and that true golf is played with the woods and the irons, but not with the putter. People think putting is a different game because the ball never gets airborne.

Whether you love or hate putting, it's a fact that if you want to play your best and score well, you need to putt your best. You cannot run away from putting, or have someone else putt for you. You must love it or learn how to love it. Our task is to help you use your mind to become a great putter.

We think putting is part art, part science, part skill, but mostly it is an act of human disposition. How you choose to think, act, and feel are the keys to using your mind to putt your best. How you handle a downhill, three-foot putt on the 18th hole to win the club championship tells others (and yourself) a lot about your personality.

We believe that putting is the most important facet of the game. The biggest challenge golfers face is their "inner" struggle on the putting green. Putting is unique because it combines a complex blend of psychological, emotional, and physical demands. You must do many things well to putt your best, but most importantly you have to think your best on the greens. We help players win their inner battle so they can win at the game of golf. Professional and amateur golfers win tournaments with great putting and great putting begins in the mind.

The physical task of putting appears simple, but every player knows that putting is more than just a physical task. When you combine the physical properties of putting with a player's personality, mental ability, and personal experience, it's not as easy as it appears. Still, it looks simple from an observer's point of view. A player uses an instrument called a putter, which is simply a metal pole with a handle and a square edge attached at the bottom. The golfer swings it back and through and propels a round ball toward a hole in the ground. This sounds simple right? But when you introduce the human element, putting turns into a test of emotional stability and human patience.

Putting truly challenges golfers, especially when golfers overread putts, steer their stroke, try too hard to execute perfectly, and see the simple task of putting as bigger than life. Its challenges bring a new light to this simple task. After three-putting from 15 feet, players are puzzled and question what happened. They walk off the green dejected, frustrated, and ego-shaken. If not dealt with, players come to accept that "the putting blues" are just part of the game. Putting woes cause even the finest players to give up, burn out, or start a desperate search for "the secret" to making putts.

What really is the secret to great putting? You won't find the answer in instructional books on stroke technique or perfect stroke path. Physical technique is part of great putting, but it's not the most important part. Nor does the answer lie within a Yoga meditation manual or an instruction booklet on relaxation exercises.

We discovered from our careers that there is only one truth to the secret of putting. The answer may surprise you. It is you. We mean your attitude and how you think, feel, and behave on the golf course. Using your mind effectively is the secret. You know what we mean because you have touched "it" on a rare occasion but couldn't hold onto "it". Everybody has had one great putting day. That one summer day when no one else was around, you found it, but it was fleeting. We can help you recover the secret, but fostering it and holding on to it rests in your hands.

This is not just a how to manual or a book on golf psychology. Our book is about the philosophy of great putting, good habits of thinking, common sense, and positive feelings. The instruction within this book comes from our experiences working with golfers of all levels, from world-class players to high-handicap amateurs. We introduce you to the same strategies we use in our work with touring professionals. This book also reflects sports psychology theory, our practice, great putters' philosophies, and common sense to help you develop better ways of thinking about the game within a game.

We suggest that you read *The Mental Art of Putting* from start to finish, but it was designed so you can read any chapter first. We hope that each time you pick it up and read it, something new will inspire you. Our goal is to give you practical and useful information that you can use right away! We have tried to keep our approach to the psychology of great putting simple and enjoyable to read. Read on and discover a new philosophy and psychology for your putting success!

Patrick J. Cohn, Ph.D. & Robert K. Winters, Ph.D.

Acknowledgments

The authors greatly appreciate the many players and coaches who shared their ideas and insights about the mental aspects of putting. We especially thank Tour professionals Bob Murphy, Larry Mize, David Edwards, Bob Estes, Greg Kraft, Bill Glasson, Bob Burns, Bernhard Langer, Jim Ferriel, Jr., Allen Miller, Meg Mallon, Helen Alfredsson, Danielle Ammaccapane, Cindy Schreyer, and Vicki Goetze for contributing their ideas. We also thank the college and ACC Golf Coaches for their contribution, especially Mike Moraghan, Willie Miller, Puggy Blackmon, Hal Morrison, and Ernie Lanford. We also appreciate Lisa Cohn, Hank Schlishberg, Adam Wienstien, John Adham, and John Mack for their reviews of earlier drafts of our book. In addition, the authors thank Dr. Robert Rotella and Dr. Herbert Price for their insights and wisdom during our careers.

Introduction

"Putting, to me, takes more guts than any other part of the game because it's mostly mental, requiring little physical ability."

Curtis Strange (1990), PGA Tour

Putting is a game within the game. It's a game played between the ears. Golf presents no greater mental challenge than your inner battle on the putting green. To putt your best, you first have to win the inner battle so you can then focus on getting the ball in the hole. The funny thing about putting is that you can have the best stroke in the world and still not be a good putter. You may be able to read greens better than anyone, but that won't help you make putts if you can't stroke a ball on line. You can have the utmost confidence in your ability to sink putts, but it doesn't matter how much confidence you have if you don't have the touch to roll a ball with the correct speed. Great putters do everything well. To putt your best, you have to read greens well, visualize how putts will react on the green, have confidence in your ability to sink putts, and trust your stroke and aim. And you have to start with the belief that you are a good putter or can become a good putter.

Putting is not and should not be technical or mechanical, but most players make it so. No one has the correct method for stroking a ball with just the right precision and effort. Most great putters, including Jack Nicklaus, agree that putting is two percent mechanics and 98 percent confidence and "touch." Larry Mize said, "When you're putting good, you're not thinking mechanics, you're thinking about picking out a line and rolling it down that line." The best putters in the world, like Jack Nicklaus, Nancy Lopez, Larry Mize, Ben Crenshaw, and Dave Stockton, have different styles of putting technique, but they all find a way to get the ball in the hole. The only similarity among great putters' methods is that they all have a stroke that is repeatable and dependable. Stroking the ball into the cup is the only thing that matters in putting—not how you get it there.

Putting is the most important part of golf because one club—the putter—is the club used most often. Golfers win most tournaments with great putting. You won't see a player win a tournament without having a good putting week. Tour players generally get the ball from tee to green in the same number of strokes. The difference between the player that finishes first and 20th is how many putts the player holes out. During a round of golf, you hit 40 to 45 percent of all shots with the putter. At the very most, you may hit 13 or 14 drives in 18 holes, but you'll hit as many as 30 to 35 putts in a round. A good amateur or professional golfer, who shoots in the low 70s, may hit 30 to 32 putts on average per round, which accounts for more strokes than all iron shots combined.

A player can recover from a wayward tee shot by hitting a good recovery shot to the green. You can also escape a poor approach shot by hitting your chip close to the pin, but you can't get a missed putt back. A putt is the last shot on every hole. There is no chance to rescue a missed putt. You can walk off a green with one, two, three, or even four putts. One-putting a green rather than three-putting translates into a big difference on the scorecard.

Good putting can save many shots during a round. You can save several shots by consistently making five- and six-foot putts for par. Other parts of your game also benefit from great putting. You don't feel you have to hit perfect shots to score well when the putter is hot, which helps you relax with the rest of your game. Good putting gives you the peace of mind and confidence that you can hit a shot off-line and still recover with a good putt.

You can also waste shots with your putter. Poor putting can pull down other parts of your game. It pressures you to improve your game with better ball-striking. When you don't putt well, you try to hit your ball or chip closer to the hole, which causes you to be overaggressive. To hit your approach shots closer to the pin, you have to hit your tee ball better. You start forcing, and overswing with your driver. You then start to overcontrol your swing and hit wayward drives.

> "Undoubtedly, the majority of present-day tournaments are decided on the putting surface."
>
> Jack Nicklaus (1976)

We wonder why golf instructors give so little attention to the psychology of putting in books, videos, and in their golf instruction. Although putting accounts for more than 40 percent of the game, most instructional books devote less than 10 percent to putting instruction, and then focus primarily on the mechanics of putting. Instructional books shy away from the most important part of putting. Any great putter will tell you that putting is mostly in the mind, but no one wants to talk about the mentality of great putting and how to think on the greens. Our book addresses this shortcoming.

The Mental Art of Putting offers a powerful method for developing a winning attitude on the greens so you can score better. In the following pages, we discuss the qualities that great putters possess, and provide a system for you to use your mind to achieve personal putting greatness. We also address how to mentally prepare for great putting, how to practice to help you score on the course, and how to create a system for warming up before a round. We also recommend practical ways to handle mental blocks or problems that plague golfers most often, such as regaining confidence, putting through spike marks, and making three-footers. Finally, we summarize the six most important keys to using your mind to putt your best, as well as how to monitor your putting progress. These mental keys to great putting include a positive attitude, putting confidence, touch and feel, total focus, vision and imagination, and trusting your stroke.

Most golfers and golf experts believe that it's not possible to make every putt you stand over. They say that to think or expect to make every putt is unrealistic, beyond human control, or just wishful thinking. We disagree. **We believe you can make every putt!** Even though you may not make every putt, you must think, act, and believe you can make every one! The abilities to read the green, see your line, visualize the path and speed of the ball, believe you can make it, and trust your line and stroke are the on-course fundamentals for using your mind to putt your best. Thinking about yourself as a good putter, visualizing making putts, practicing effectively, and using positive self-talk are the off-course fundamentals for using your mind to putt your best.

We don't pretend that great thinking or a great attitude is a substitute for practicing your putting. A great mindset won't offset an inconsistent putting stroke. You must be able to start the ball on your intended line. More confidence and a better attitude will help you score better on the greens, but they do not replace the ability to repeat a stroke and improve your touch and feel through quality practice. However, when you combine physical practice with a strong mental approach, you fill yourself with positive putting enthusiasm and this is a great place to start if you want to be a great putter. This is what *The Mental Art of Putting* is all about. When you blend the mental art of putting with physical skill, your confidence and putting performance are sure to improve. Have fun using your mind to putt your best!

Lagman or Charger? Determining Your Putting Style

Most great players in the world—people like Jack Nicklaus and Arnold Palmer—have a well-defined philosophy about how to approach putting. Whether you are a professional or an amateur, you too should have a philosophy of putting to guide your behavior on the course. It's like having a game plan. Football teams develop an approach to how they will play a particular game, which they base on each team's strengths and weaknesses. The team then carries out a game plan and stays with it to achieve the greatest consistency and success. You too, need to develop your game plan for success on the putting green.

TWO DIFFERENT STYLES OF PUTTING

Most players have one of two basic philosophies of putting. One style of putting is aggressive, with the player "charging" the cup and hitting the ball into the back of the hole, keeping the ball on its intended line. Another style is the "die" or lag method of putting. A player using this style hits the ball with just enough speed to "die" the ball into the front or side of the cup.

Now, let's examine these two styles of putting and see which one best fits your game.

An aggressive-style putter thinks, "never up, never in" and strokes putts boldly enough to hold them on line. This type of putter does not worry about making a two- or three-foot putt coming back if the ball misses the hole. Conversely, a lag putter uses gravity to increase the chances of the ball falling into the hole. Simple physics dictates that a ball is more likely to drop into the hole when it rolls over the lip of the cup if it is moving slower. Putts that are moving faster when they hit the side of the cup are not as likely to fall into the hole. The advantages of lag putting are: (1) if a putt hits a part of the hole, it has a better chance of going in, and (2) if you miss, it will be closer to the cup. Usually, a lag putter will have an easier second putt because the ball stops closer to the cup. The disadvantage of lag putting is that it is harder for a ball to stay on its intended line when traveling slower. Thus, on bumpy or spiked greens the ball will lose its line easier and stray off course.

> "I've never seen a ball that's left three feet short of the hole go in—but then again, I've never seen one that goes by three feet go in either."
>
> Jim Colbert, Senior PGA Tour

DO YOU LAG OR CHARGE?

Some great putters like Nicklaus, Ben Crenshaw, and Tom Kite advocate lag putting, whereas other great players like Arnold Palmer, Tom Watson, and Greg Norman stick to the "charge" style of putting. The approach a player adopts usually depends on his or her personality, general style of play, and mental approach to the game. Players who are generally aggressive with other aspects of their game usually carry that style of play into their short game. If

Understanding your putting style provides you with a putting game plan.

you play aggressively like Greg Norman or John Daly, and shoot at pins tucked behind bunkers, cut the corners of doglegs on your tee shot, and go for par five's in two, you most likely putt with the same boldness. You take more risks that might lead to good scoring, but you also run the risk of shooting some high numbers when the gamble doesn't pay off. If you putt aggressively, you must have confidence in your ability to make the putt coming back. The "charge" method is a live-and-die-by-the-sword attitude.

> "I think you should decide whether you are by nature or choice a 'charge' or 'die' putter."
>
> Jack Nicklaus (1974), Senior PGA Tour

More conservative players, who hit three woods and irons off the tee, play for the middle of the green on approach shots, and lay-up on par five holes, most likely will have the same approach on the green. A deliberate and calculating player like Nicklaus avoids the risk of hitting the ball too far past the hole. Again, there is a tradeoff. A conservative player does not take as many chances, but he may not get into trouble as much as an aggressive player. Lag putters most likely leave some putts short of the cup, but they probably three-putt less than aggressive putters.

In some situations, a die putter must charge the hole and a charge putter must lag the ball to the hole. On shorter putts, a die putter may need to hit a putt firm enough to take out any break and "hold" the ball on its line. Similarly, on very fast greens or when playing long, downhill putts, a charge putter may need to lag putt.

THE IMPORTANCE OF SPEED

Short game expert Dave Pelz (1989) suggests that players should hit putts with enough speed so they travel 17 inches past the hole. He says that a putt has the best chance of going in the hole when hit with the correct speed to carry it through the "lumpy donut". The lumpy donut is a circular area around the hole that becomes bumpy from previous players who have left foot print impressions. Pelz's 17-inch rule holds up well under average green speeds, but it changes drastically if you are putting on very fast, smooth greens or very slow, bumpy greens or on greens with severe slopes. On very smooth bent grass greens, the distance shortens to 10 to 12 inches past the hole. This suggests that a lag putter may be missing more putts because the ball is moving too slowly near the hole. However, 17 inches is not a "gimme" for a player who lacks confidence. And if you putt boldly on fast greens, you sometimes have a five- or six-foot putt coming back.

WHAT IS YOUR ATTITUDE ABOUT PUTTING?

Are you excited about getting on the green and knocking in the putt or do you begin to tighten up when you pull the putter out of your bag due to the fear of three-putting? Your general attitude about putting influences the philosophy you will adopt. A player who fears three-putting and doesn't want to grind over a three-foot putt coming back will most likely adopt the die method because it's easier on his nerves to leave the ball close enough for a tap-in.

An aggressive player like Greg Norman doesn't worry about having to make a three-footer coming back. He accepts the risk of rolling the ball past the hole to give himself a better chance of making the putt. He is confident that he will make the next putt no matter where the ball stops. This attitude says "go for it" and accept what happens.

> "If you entertain the possibility of a 'next' putt, you're not focusing on sinking the one you have."
>
> Greg Norman (1988), PGA Tour

Develop a putting philosophy for making putts instead of wishing putts!

Norman (1988) says there are several good reasons for putting aggressively. First, you will improve your chances of making putts if you don't leave as many putts short. Second, a firm stroke allows you to accelerate through the ball, imparting a better spin on the ball. Third, on short putts, an aggressive stroke lets you play your ball straight at the hole, taking out any break that may influence the roll. For long putts, bold putting helps you see how the ball reacts as it passes the hole, giving you a better indication of the break for the next putt. Lastly, it can be frustrating to hit putts that stop short of the hole. It's disappointing when you did everything right except judging the correct speed and leave it short. You know the putt would have dropped if you had just hit it a little firmer. And the frustration from leaving them short but on-line can certainly try your patience.

FINDING YOUR STYLE

Whatever method you subscribe to, stick with what you believe and what works for you. If you worry about hitting the ball four feet past the hole, an aggressive style of putting may not be for you. If you hate to leave the ball short of the cup, lag putting may not be right for you. Your philosophy will also depend on your personality. If you have an assertive, confident attitude, you're more likely to adopt the charge method of putting. Lag putting may be better for you if you are a more conservative or strategic player. Remember, there are other factors that decide how boldly you putt. On faster greens or ones with more slope, it is dangerous to putt boldly. You also have to consider factors such as your position in a match. You don't want to roll the ball four feet past the cup if you need to make par to win the match.

Try This!

Next time you are on the practice green, hit a few 20-foot putts at different speeds. First, die a few putts in the hole and then switch to charging some putts. See what style feels comfortable and discover how many putts you make with each style. Don't try to smash your putts three feet past the hole. Do the same thing with five-foot putts and test which style is most effective. Use the style that will allow you to make the most putts. Then, use the philosophy or style that works best for you on the practice green. Commit to this style of putting for an entire 18 holes and then chart your progress for at least three more rounds.

The Best of the Best: Qualities of Great Putters

Our work with and study of great putters reveals that they think differently about putting than average or mediocre putters do. To be an exceptional putter you must have a repeatable stroke and, most importantly, a great attitude about putting. A great attitude is not just a positive attitude. A great attitude is thinking you are a good putter, trusting your method, relying on feel rather than mechanics, and knowing how to get the ball into the hole. In addition, you must have total confidence, a strong desire to practice and improve, and the ability to aim and align yourself to a target.

This chapter focuses on the mindset and personality of great putters. To be a good putter, you must have the complete package and do several things well. Great putters are more decisive, have more confidence in their ability to make putts, and understand how to get the ball into the hole. They also believe they are great putters, love to putt, focus more on getting the ball into the hole than on missing, and can easily forget about missed putts. PGA Tour player Bob Estes says that great putters do most things well:

> Great putters have everything. . . . The speed is good, you are getting it on line, you are seeing the breaks, you are reading the greens, you are confident and comfortable with your touch on the greens. I don't think you can separate those things and be considered a great putter.

DO YOU THINK OF YOURSELF AS A GOOD PUTTER?

Great putters have a totally different mindset that separates them from average putters. What is the difference? All great putters believe they are great putters. Average or poor putters defeat themselves before they reach the putting surface because they see themselves as bad putters. These players remember only the putts they missed and forget the ones they made.

Great putters not only believe they are good putters but also become excited about making putts. They truly believe they can make every putt. Mediocre putters think of themselves as "OK" or streaky putters. This negative attitude causes them to focus more on how many they miss and makes them wonder how they will make the next putt. They worry more about three-putting instead of finding a way to get the ball into the hole.

> "Good putters know they are good—that is the way you have to think."
>
> Willie Miller, Furman University Golf Coach

Attitude Differences between Good and Poor Putters

Great Attitude	Poor Attitude
• Views self as a great putter	• Views self as a poor putter
• Loves to putt	• Fears and hates putting
• Has high self-confidence	• Has low self-confidence
• Trusts decisions	• Changes mind often
• Focuses better with pressure	• Becomes scared and anxious
• Thinks mechanics aren't vital	• Focuses on mechanics
• Understands one's method	• Tries to prefect stroke
• Can visualize well	• Cannot visualize well
• Plays with positive emotions	• Plays with negative emotions
• Lets it happen	• Tries too hard
• Simplifies putting	• Makes putting complex
• Lets go of mistakes	• Dwells on mistakes
• Practices to make putts	• Practices stroke mechanics

ARE YOU CONFIDENT IN YOUR ABILITY?

The best putters in the world have an enormous amount of confidence in their ability to make putts. When Lee Trevino or Dave Stockton step onto the green, they have a mindset that allows them to think they can make every putt. They never entertain doubts about missing. The statistical probability of making a 20-foot putt is considerably less than making it, but that doesn't enter a great putter's mind—he or she is thinking only about making the putt. Great putters do not have a "missing" mindset.

> "The most important thing is to have confidence in what you are doing."
>
> Tom Kite (1990)

> **Great putters are excited about putting and "see" themselves putting well.**

Many players lose confidence when they miss a couple of putts early in the round. Great putters don't lose confidence when they miss early because they know the putts will eventually fall. They are more patient than other putters. A poor putter will give up and stop trying early. This person says, "It just isn't my day." This is a self-fulfilling prophecy. Poor putters talk themselves into thinking that they can't make putts. Throwing in the towel protects their egos. For this player, it's easier to cope with poor putting if he or she stops trying to make them.

Average putters don't believe in their ability on the putting green. At times, they may feel confident, but confidence comes and goes with how many putts they make. An average putter starts the day thinking he can make putts and when he misses early, that confidence dwindles fast and is lost for the day. When confidence dwindles for a streaky putter, it is hard to recover.

ARE YOU A DOUBTER?

One characteristic of good putting is decisiveness. A player who continually changes his mind on the putting surface is prone to be a doubter. Being decisive means making decisions and carrying decisions out without second-guessing yourself. Great putters are very resolute. They have an exact plan about how to go about sinking putts. They pick a line and decide how they are going to hit the putt and stay committed to that plan. They don't allow doubt or indecision to influence their actions. If they do have doubt about missing a putt, they know how to deal with it and can refocus on making the putt.

> "You have to believe you are going to make the putt before you hit it, and be precise on how you are going to hit it."
>
> Vicki Goetze, LPGA Tour

An average putter will doubt his or her decisions and change his or her mind often. A doubter has a hard time making a good stroke because he or she hasn't decided how the ball will react on the green and how he or she will get it into the hole. It's hard to hit a solid putt without a clear idea of what you are trying to do.

DO YOU BELIEVE IN YOUR METHOD?

Many players lose their effectiveness on the green by trying too hard to perfect their stroke. If you have a mechanical flaw, you need to improve your mechanics. But if you think you must have perfect mechanics to putt well, you may never reach your putting potential. A player who worries more about mechanics and developing a perfect stroke, practices their golf stroke and doesn't *play* golf.

> "Good putters make a commitment to hit the ball, they don't think about stroke, stroke is a paralyzing word, they think about hitting the ball."
>
> Bob Murphy, Senior PGA Tour

Great putters are not technique-oriented—they don't putt mechanically. They rely on touch and feel. They learn to get the ball into the hole without thinking about "how to" get the ball into the hole. Great putters understand their method and have faith that it works for them. No matter how technically sound a great putter's stroke is, he or she knows that it is repeatable and that it works. You see many different putting strokes on the pro tours, but they are all functional because each player trusts his or her stroke and is consistent from shot to shot. Players like Lee Trevino, Tom Watson, Ben Crenshaw, and Dave Stockton stroke the ball differently, but they are all successful because they have enormous confidence and truly know their method works for them.

DO YOU PRACTICE FOR TOUCH?

Great putters talk a lot about the importance of having "soft hands". Soft hands means having light grip pressure, which allows you to feel your putter head and get reliable feedback about the "solidness" of contact from your putter. Great putters have excellent touch and feel on the greens. Many good putters, like Jack Nicklaus, believe great putting is mostly having good feel or touch and has little to do with mechanics. A few players think you are born with good feel and touch, and it can improve only so much with practice. Most players believe that feel and touch develop through practice and repetition. LPGA standout Meg Mallon learned how to develop touch through practice and a routine. She said, "When I learned how to read a putt and how to have a routine, then I could develop feel and the touch because once I knew I was set-up correctly, I could go ahead and stroke it."

No matter how much of feel or touch is inborn, most great putters rely on specific drills to improve their touch. The level of touch and feel you develop ultimately depends on how you practice to improve touch.

> **To putt your best, you must rely more on your human genius than a mechanical approach.**

"Most good putters have good touch and feel because putting is a lot more than stroking the ball toward the cup. You have to have good feel to be a good putter."

Larry Mize, PGA Tour

CAN YOU SEE THE LINE?

Any good putter will tell you that the ability to "see" the line or visualize the ball rolling along the green is critical to good putting. The ability to visualize is important to all facets of the game but it may be the most critical in putting. What is the first thing you look at when you read a putt? Reading a putt on a sloped green takes imagination and the capability to see the line or path of the putt in your mind's eye. Setting up and aiming at a target also requires the ability to picture how the ball reacts on the green. Great putters like Larry Mize rely on their imagination and have the ability to envision how a ball reacts on the green, depending on the slope, speed, and type of grass.

Two factors are crucial to putting: distance (speed) and direction (target). Both require good vision. You must have good depth perception and distance judgment to accurately see how far away you are from the target. You also must aim yourself correctly with the target. To do both, you must first "see" the line of your putt.

DO YOU LOVE TO PUTT?

One of the strongest emotions in golf is fear. Fear comes in many forms such as the fear of failure, the fear of embarrassment, or just the fear of missing a putt. When fear takes over, you're done. But the emotion of controlled excitement is very useful. Excitement is a positive emotion that helps you focus and gives you energy. Fear is a negative emotion that diverts your attention and drains your energy.

Great putters step on the green with excitement. They focus on how to make the putt. Their excitement is transformed into positive energy that helps them concentrate during their preshot routines. Poor putters become scared when they step on the putting green. They think about how they must avoid three-putting. The fear of missing the putt turns into negative thinking, which causes many players to miss putts.

> "Most makeable putts are missed because of fear or a negative attitude, not because of faulty technique per se."
>
> Jack Nicklaus (1974)

DO YOU GIVE YOUR BEST EFFORT?

Most players think that the harder you try to make a putt, the better you will putt. This is not always the case. You hurt your ability to make putts when you overanalyze your read, try too hard, or overcontrol your stroke. Overworking your read causes you to second-guess your decisions. Trying too hard can cause you to think too much about the line and then forget the speed of the putt or think too much about the speed and forget direction. Overcontrolling your stroke ruins your ability to stroke the ball smoothly and effortlessly.

> "It's easy to try to be too perfect in golf and especially in putting and that's a very tense way to putt for me."
>
> Larry Mize, PGA Tour

Great putters know how to give their best effort, not the most effort. They don't tie themselves in knots by overanalyzing or trying too hard. Great putters focus on their routine and allow experience and instinct to take over. They know how to get into the flow and become immersed in the requirements of the task. A good putter naturally reads the putt, aligns to the target automatically, and instinctively focuses on the hole or the line of the putt.

DO YOU KNOW THAT YOU'RE NOT PERFECT?

Great putters don't get down or frustrated when they miss putts. They realize it's not humanly possible to make every putt. The best players don't become upset after missing one or two putts because they know that they will make the next one. Often, a good putter like Lee Trevino blames a missed putt on an imperfection in the green, a spike mark, or a poorly cut hole, rather than on himself. If he blames something that he has no control over, his confidence is not affected negatively.

Great putters accept that they will have good days and bad days. They understand the fact that they are human and they can't putt well everyday. If they putt poorly one day, they know the next day will be different. Poor putters get upset with themselves and berate their putting ability when they miss. This type of player's negative reaction reinforces his or her notion of being a poor putter. He or she says, "If only I could putt, I would be a good player."

DO YOU PRACTICE TO MAKE PUTTS?

Great putters know how to get the most out of their practice. They practice to make putts, which helps them succeed on the golf course. Great putters practice to make every putt, anywhere. They give full concentration to make each putt as if they are putting on the golf course. Average putters practice their strokes instead of practice to make putts. They try to hit as many putts as they can in a given time. They don't hit each putt with full intention and focus.

Mind Matters

How do you perceive your putting ability? Do you think you are a good putter, a poor putter, or an average putter? Does your image of yourself as a putter change with the level of your play or amount of practice? Think back to a time you had a good image of yourself as a putter. What did you think about your putting? What helped you think you were a good putter? What experiences helped you feel confident? Try to recall what you were feeling and thinking about. Relive a round when you putted your best. Experience yourself playing with confidence and putting very well the next round you play.

Try This!

Think back to both your positive and negative experiences with putting. In one column, write down the positive characteristics that you possess as a putter. In the other column, write down the negative characteristics you possess. Commit yourself to building your positive characteristics and changing your negative traits. Do this, and you are on your way to becoming a better putter.

A Healthy Start: Choosing the I-Can-Make-Everything Attitude

Attitude is the most misunderstood and overlooked concept in golf. No matter what your age, gender, or playing experience, a positive attitude is vital to shooting low numbers and playing better. Great putters recognize the impact of positive thoughts and feelings on their putting success. A positive attitude on the greens is the first step on the way to great putting. However, a great attitude doesn't come easily or soon enough for most golfers. Great dreams of golfing success are often never realized due to a negative attitude caused by images of missed putts, lip-outs, and three-putts.

CHOOSING A GOOD ATTITUDE

Webster's Dictionary defines attitude as: "A mental position or feeling in regard to something." Another popular definition is: "One's feeling or perspective about something that supports those feelings." To putt and play well, a golfer must first understand the importance of a positive putting attitude. What is your definition of a great putting attitude? (Stop here and think about your last round). Did your attitude **help** or **hurt** your performance on the green? As you read on, develop your own definition of a positive putting attitude.

The power of your mind is unlimited. Mostly everyone who plays golf has similar brain power and neurological functioning. Those persons who use their minds to its full potential become successful, regardless of their professional endeavors. Everyone who plays golf can develop a great attitude. You start your day (or round) with the ability to choose your attitude. The game then becomes a competition of you against the golf course and your inner battle. To take your game to a higher level, you must use your mind to help you play better by deciding to have a positive attitude.

> "The greatest discovery of my generation is that a human being can alter his life by altering his attitudes of mind."
>
> William James (John-Roger, 1989),
> Father of Modern Psychology

People do have the power to control their destiny. But many people don't take responsibility for achieving their dreams. This is especially true in putting. Many golfers talk themselves out of their putting skill. If golfers could learn to putt free without fear, without self-criticism, they would enjoy putting and putt better. A positive and supportive attitude is a big advantage for a player, especially when there is substantial "pressure" to produce.

What is the first thing that comes to mind about your putting? Is your putting attitude supportive and helpful? Is it positive and uplifting? Or is your attitude filled with negative thoughts and feelings of missed putts? If this is the case, you might be in need of an attitude overhaul. Do you find yourself doubting your ability to make a pressure putt for the club championship? Do you have the confidence to make a putt by your willpower alone? Putting is the great equalizer in the sport of golf. Putting is what separates the men from the boys and the lionhearted from the gutless.

A STUDY IN ATTITUDE

All golfers, at one time or another, face self-doubt and anxiety when putting in the heat of competition. Many players tell us that their attitude can change on the success or failure of a single putt. For example, there was a great player in the 1940s and '50s named Ivan Gantz who displayed a volcanic temper on the putting green. Once, Ivan missed a putt less than two feet in length. He would smack himself in the jaw with clenched fists and if that was not enough, he would throw his putter high into the air and stood underneath waiting for it to come crashing down on his head. If the falling putter didn't hit him, he would go through the same ritual and punish himself again. This not only happened once, but several times. He was given the nicknames "Crazy Ivan" and "Ivan the Terrible."

What is sad, but true, about this colorful story is that Ivan Gantz was one of his era's most talented players. But Ivan never reached the star potential of a Snead, Demaret, or Hogan, even though he defeated them on occasion. Who knows how many golf tournaments Ivan could have won if he had gained control over his emotions and developed a positive putting attitude. Years later, Ivan reflected on his career and said, "If I could have kept my emotions under control and been willing to work half as hard on my attitude as I did on my swing and the rest of the game, I would have taken a lot more green and gold home, instead of frustration and heartache."

> "Take charge of your own attitude. Don't let anyone else choose it for you."
>
> H. Jackson Brown Jr. (1991), Author/Philosopher

MAKING THE RIGHT CHOICE

A key to developing a healthy putting attitude is choosing to have a positive attitude. Many players start with an OK attitude, but then as the round progresses, it becomes negative. These players make the mistake of letting others choose an attitude for them, and it is often negative. How often have you played with your friends and someone said, "Gosh, you're putting terrible today!" Or they say, "Wow, you just can't buy a putt today, can you?" How did this affect your confidence? If you said that it didn't affect your performance or you don't let other people affect you, great! However, for some players, this hurts their confidence, and their chances of making putts that day are seriously impaired. Often, players take what others tell them as the ultimate truth.

This scenario happens everyday on the athletic fields, playgrounds, and golf courses, but this needn't happen to you. It starts when Mr. or Ms. "Bad Attitude" project their "putting negativism" onto you, and before you know it, you accept their attitude and putt as poorly as they do.

In sport psychology, we call this "psyching yourself out." In this situation, you need to create a wall between you and the negative input from other people. Keep reminding yourself about the good things that are yet to happen on the putting green. You have to think that eventually the putts will drop, that you will win the battle over your thoughts, and ultimately, build a great putting attitude.

You are responsible for developing and reinforcing a good attitude. You must remain unaffected by what others say about your putting or technique. If you take others' negative comments to heart, you internalize their negativity. The famous college basketball coach John Wooden said, "The only difference between success and failure is the acknowledgment that success or failure is self-determined, and that successful people are the only ones that acknowledge it to be so."

THE GOLDEN ATTITUDE

If there is one "secret" to great putting, it is this: you must get into each putt with complete intention and concentration, have a specific plan or strategy in mind, believe in your ability, then putt the ball where you want it to go, and accept the result.

"Decide what you are going to do, then go ahead and do it."

Bobby Locke (Palmer, 1986), Putting Great

This type of thinking is what we call "The Golden Attitude." This attitude proposes that with each new putt, you fill yourself with enthusiasm, hopefulness, positive expectation, and belief in your ability that you will be successful. Implementing "The Golden Attitude" on every shot allows you to totally focus on "the now and the new" versus "the old and the bad." It also helps you focus on the process of making putts instead of derailing yourself with previously missed putts and lip-outs. Just imagine how good your putting would be if every time you had the feeling that "This one's going in" or "This is the putt that gets me going!" How much better would you putt if you always thought this way?

Touring professionals are the first people to say that they constantly try to capture the elusive feeling of self-confidence, particularly in putting. In our work with professional and amateur players, we always look for keys that will unlock their playing potential. When they putt poorly, the words "low confidence" always come up. Confidence and belief in oneself are necessary for performing at peak potential.

> "One of the most important things in putting is confidence. You can't stand over a putt and think you can't make it if you want to make it."
>
> Danielle Ammaccapane, LPGA Tour

One of the most important performance statistics, next to money earned on the PGA Tour, is average number of putts per round. This supports that the adage "Drive for show, putt for dough" is not just an over-used cliche, but an important piece of the mental game of golf. But we think the most important statistic, if you could measure it, is confidence.

It's sad that many would-be-great golfers (and putters) tarnish their putting with negative thinking. Most players put so much pressure on themselves to make putts it becomes a do-or-die situation. When you adopt "The Golden Attitude," every putt becomes a new experience and the adage "one shot at a time" becomes simple to follow. Make a commitment to the philosophy that on every putt you are going to give 100 percent effort, then live with the results no matter what happens! This way of thinking is hard to commit to, but when you accept it, you will begin to turn your putting around.

Usually, players start a round with a positive attitude, but tend to self-destruct after a few missed putts. At first, they are filled with positive thoughts and confidence, but then abandon those thoughts and feelings when they miss early or if they don't reach their expectations. Using "The Golden Attitude" and armed with a positive mindset, you *can* putt your best.

THE POWER OF WORDS

Developing a new attitude involves learning to describe yourself, and situations you are part of, using positive words. Words can be healing bandages or wounding daggers because the type of message you send yourself influences your attitude. We all talk to ourselves often during a round, and this is called self-talk. The words you choose to use can be either positive or negative. On the putting green, do you use positive self-talk to support yourself or negative self-talk to criticize the outcome or your effort?

Monitor what you say to yourself for one full day. See just how positive or negative you are with yourself. If you were on the 18th green putting for a birdie to win your club championship, do you say to yourself, "OK, this putt is just like all the others that I've putted today and I'm putting well, so this one is going in, too!" Or do you say, "Don't screw this one up, you screwed up too many of these in the past!"

Negative self-talk is a time bomb waiting to explode. It plants the seed for failure and self-doubt. The type of words you use may not hurt your putting immediately, but eventually, the seeds of negativism begin to erode your confidence. (We discuss negative thinking and fear of failure in Chapter 9.) The truth is, words influence our behavior. You change behavior positively when you talk to yourself in a "listener friendly" language. You help yourself when you say, "It's OK, hang in there, the putts will drop!" Or "Come on now, you're doing

> **What you say to yourself before you putt often determines your success or failure.**

everything right, just stay patient and focus on this putt!" This is what helps you tolerate mediocre putting days. Also, words that are positive in tone and meaning help us to be more patient and composed. Patience and composure help us to relax and focus more effectively. Start a cycle of good feelings by using words that plant seeds of confidence and success.

THE LITTLE ENGINE: A RELEVANT CHILDREN'S STORY

Do you remember the children's bedtime story, "The Little Engine That Could"? It is about building a positive attitude. It goes like this: There was once a little engine who wanted to be accepted by his peers. No one in the train depot gave him a chance, nor did anyone give him credit for being a locomotive. One day, the other trains were out of service and an important assignment came into the depot. The Little Engine's task was to make it over a huge mountain and take packages of supplies to people on the other side. On the way, the Little Engine started having doubts about his ability to make it over the huge mountain. He started thinking to himself, "Who am I to think that I can make it over this mountain, when the other larger and more experienced trains can't even make it?" This type of thinking persisted until the Little Engine finally thought, "Maybe, I can do it!" The Little Engine said to himself, "I think I can, I think I can!" This helped motivate himself to climb the big mountain. On and on, the Little Engine climbed, always reminding himself that he could do it. Even when he wanted to give up, he refused to succumb to self-doubt. Before he knew it, the Little Engine had reached the summit and was on the other side of the Great Mountain, rushing onward to save the day.

The lesson of the story is that a positive attitude gives you a chance to make progress toward your desired goal. How many times have you been "The Little Engine" and no one gave you a chance or thought you had the "right stuff" to accomplish great things? Once you decide to use the words "I can," you give yourself the privilege of at least trying. The will to say "I can" provides you with a starting point to build long-lasting putting success.

When golfers use the words "I can't," what they are really saying is: "I won't" or "I won't give myself an opportunity to try to be successful." Poor putters use excuses such as: "I can't putt!" or "These greens are too bumpy," or

"These greens are too fast," or any number of explanations for expecting failure. These players never give themselves any opportunity to putt their best. Use the words "I can," rather than "I can't" and give yourself an opportunity to build a positive attitude.

DEVELOPING THE I-CAN-MAKE-EVERYTHING ATTITUDE

The first thing people ask is, "What can I do to make more putts?" or "How do I become a more confident putter?" We don't pretend to have a quick fix, but one thing is certain, unless you start with a mindset that helps you make **something** during a round of golf, you won't ever give yourself a chance of climbing out of the trenches and becoming a good putter. If you can be excited about putting again and truly believe that you can and want to improve, then you are moving in the direction of putting success.

The theory of "Try to make everything" is really a great putting theory. However, for those who putt poorly and think they lack talent, then the adage of "Let's make everything" probably won't work. Your putting subconscious is not ready to accept the idea of "Let's make everything" and you're not going to hole putts. As Bob Toski, a respected golf teacher, says: "You can eat an elephant, but you need to do it one bite at a time."

Before you can make "everything," you need to make "something," or at least make a few. You have to practice making putts, seeing putts go into the hole repeatedly, and using positive self-talk. Reinforce good putting by noting your improvement. You do this by building memories of successful putting experiences and depositing them into your memory bank. This may mean making putts no longer than two feet. The best way to start is by building on successful experiences. Build momentum, begin with two footers and then move to longer putts of three, four, and five feet to reinforce the idea that you can make putts.

> **Depositing successful putting pictures into your memory bank pays off big dividends on the course!**

By adopting a mindset that says "I am on my way to better putting," you develop an attitude that flows into other areas of your game. Start today. Right now. Give yourself the privilege to adopt "The Golden Attitude" about your putting. Use confident, positive words that accentuate your strengths. Tell yourself that today you have decided to become the best putter that you can possibly be! Remember, all great putters constantly remind themselves that they can putt, even when the putts don't fall into the cup.

Try This!

Commit yourself to the idea that you are going to improve your attitude today. Monitor the type of words you use to describe yourself and your situation. Use only positive and reinforcing words whenever you talk of or think about your putting. Never complain about the greens or your putting stroke. Imagine making putts every day (even when you aren't playing). Make putting easier by focusing on the task of stroking the ball. Forget about missing or making. Remember only the putts that lip-in, never the ones that lip-out!

The One-Putt Mindset: The Only Way to Think

In every sport, whether it's football, basketball, baseball, or golf, successful athletes always speak of the importance of self-confidence. People with self-confidence trust and believe in themselves, which is visible in how they carry themselves. Top athletes possess special physical and mental abilities and have high expectations for excellence. If there is one common thread to superior sport achievement, it is an athlete's self-confidence in his or her ability.

David Hemery (1986) interviewed 63 top athletes in several sports, including golfing great Arnold Palmer, to study the common attributes of high achieving athletes. Hemery found that 86 percent of athletes said that self-confidence is the single greatest advantage they have over other athletes. Sport psychology consultant Dr. Tom Hanson (1992) interviewed five of the all-time greatest hitters in baseball to understand what separates them from their fellow competitors. Each ballplayer's view of how they achieve success differs, but one common thread was total self-confidence and belief in one's own ability, day after day, season after season.

All athletes strive to gain an "edge" over the competition and train to instill a sense of personal mastery and competence, but confidence can be fleeting for many. When one has confidence, it can be a tremendous asset in competition, as well as in every other area of human existence, but when one loses it, it can be devastating. Confidence is the name of the game in superior athletic performance.

CONFIDENCE: THE NAME OF THE GAME

Golf is similar to other sports in that performance changes with an athlete's level of self-confidence. Most people forget that golfers are athletes who perform in an environment that is continually changing day to day. Golfers have the challenge of playing on different courses with different playing and weather conditions. Golfers are also human beings who are subject to distractions, psychological pressures, and unique challenges that other sports don't possess. Athletes from other sports who play golf say that golf is the most difficult game they have ever played because of its intense psychological and physical demands.

A particular psychological challenge is to play golf with a consistently high level of self-confidence. Any veteran player will say that maintaining self-confidence is the biggest battle in golf. Winning this battle is even more important on the putting greens.

> "You can have the purest putting stroke in the world, but if you don't have confidence in it, it's not going to produce the desired results."
>
> Tom Kite (1990), PGA Tour

Confidence is a term that means many things to many people. If you ask 10 golfers to define confidence, you might get 10 different variations ranging from trust to believing in oneself to strength of conviction, and so on. To some, confidence is a global concept, like thinking you can do anything and do it well. To others, high confidence implies that they can accomplish a certain task. Either view is accurate, but most sport psychologists define confidence as the belief in one's ability to accomplish a task. True confidence is the kind of confidence that says you truly know that you will be successful in making putts.

Golfers often talk about feeling confident and letting it show, but enduring confidence comes from being successful and producing desired results. A person must have some successful performances to feel confident. Achievement is the backbone of a player's self-confidence. Nothing builds confidence quicker than success. Confidence increases when there is something of value riding on the outcome and you succeed.

Confidence is a cyclical process. But where does the cycle begin and how do you build self-confidence? Which comes first, great putting or high self-confidence? Have you ever heard of the chicken or the egg story? Unless you can start with a putting mindset that says "I know I can putt" or "I want to believe in myself and my putting," you aren't likely to give yourself a chance at improving.

According to renowned sport psychology consultant Dr. Bob Rotella (1986), putting confidence isn't something that starts from the outside and works its way inside. Rather, it starts from the inside and manifests itself outwardly via holed putts and successful performances on the putting green, which then makes you more confident. PGA Tour player Donnie Hammond thinks that you have to believe in yourself before you can make putts. He said "To start putting well, you need to make putts, but what helps you to start making putts is to tell yourself that 'I'm a good putter, I should be making putts.' Then you start making putts and the more putts you make, the more confidence you have."

What if you needed an important putt to win a local tournament or reach your best score ever? Most players would say "I'll become confident only if I make this putt!" Instead, those same players would benefit from the philosophy that says you are already a good putter and that you are going to do everything you can to ensure that your putt is going in the cup. Selecting a plan, focusing on performance cues, committing yourself to a plan and stroking the ball with determination, are the keys to giving yourself a chance. Or the other option is to continue fighting the demons of incompetence and hopelessness. With this approach, you are self-empowered. Great putting begins with building and reinforcing confidence within yourself and transferring that inner strength to your putting performance on the green.

COMPETENCE AND THE PUTTING CYCLE: IT WORKS BOTH WAYS!

We've previously said that nothing breeds confidence like success. Putting confidence is a revolving cycle. The cycle starts with the player believing in himself and his putting stroke and trusting what he practiced. When a stroke is "overlearned" through practice it leads to competence. Competence is vitally important to the putting confidence cycle because it translates into confidence on the greens. Putting competence is a mastery of physical ability to sink a putt or lag a fifty-foot putt close for a "gimme."

Putting competence also includes the ability to aim the putter face correctly and stroke the ball solidly on your intended line. Psychological putting competence includes the ability to read greens, judge breaks, have a feel for distance and speed, and creatively visualize the entire process. These components of putting competence are vital for developing confidence in your putting. In golf, confidence and competence may be inseparable, but competence is the foundation for confidence.

THE POSITIVE PUTTING CYCLE

The positive putting cycle starts with a basic belief in your ability to putt well, no matter how good or bad a putter you are. This belief starts a positive practice plan. As you practice, you develop competence in your putting skills. Effective putting practice develops and reinforces psychological and physical putting competence. When you begin to make putts on the course, you develop confidence in putting. As your confidence increases, you gain positive feelings, which further establishes your belief in yourself as a good putter. The positive cycle continues, which increases the chance of future success. This cycle travels in a positive direction even when you fail to make putts.

> "Confidence comes from making putts. You have to have success in sinking putts. You have to have positive results."
>
> Bill Glasson, PGA Tour

Self-confident players always find ways to continue on a positive putting cycle. If the putts do not fall, a positive player reminds himself to stay patient and know that his effort will pay off eventually. Confident players use positive self-talk and tell themselves that they are "due" to make putts. This helps them resist becoming negative and cynical due to a lack of falling putts.

In other sports, such as basketball, coaches talk of the "shooter's mentality." This idea says that a ballplayer on a cold streak who keeps shooting and

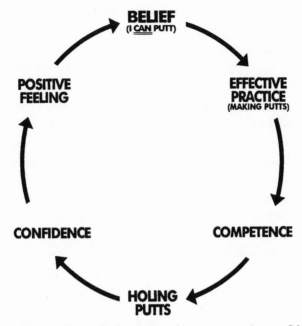

BELIEF
(I CAN PUTT)

EFFECTIVE PRACTICE
(MAKING PUTTS)

POSITIVE FEELING

COMPETENCE

CONFIDENCE

HOLING PUTTS

The Positive Putting Cycle develops and improves putting confidence.

doing the right things fundamentally will eventually get his "shooter's eye" back. Ask any college or professional coach or player, and they'll tell you that the player who doesn't want to shoot or quits shooting is the one who will be sitting on the bench.

The same is true in golf. If Ben Crenshaw finds that he is not making putts, do you think he says to himself, "I guess I just don't have the touch today, so I guess I'll just stop trying?" Do great putters just throw in the towel because they didn't get immediate results? Hardly. They have a shooter's mentality, which allows them to aim the putter, fire away, and go on to the next putt believing they can make it despite missing on previous attempts. Great putters receive positive feedback from putts that fall just short of the hole by telling themselves: "That one was just one roll short of perfection," versus negative thinkers who say "I left another one short." Confident putters think, feel, and act in ways to maintain confidence on the greens. Players who lack confidence find any excuse to fail.

"If it is a positive, you use it. If it is a negative, you throw it out."

Vicki Goetze, LPGA Tour

THE NEGATIVE PUTTING CYCLE

However, if success breeds success, we also can say that nothing destroys putting confidence faster than missing and failing to see any positive pictures. Continual failure destroys a player inside until any residue of confidence and previous mastery experiences erode. In a negative putting cycle, a player starts with little, if any, belief in him or herself as a putter. This leads to no practice or ineffective practice. Instead of developing confidence, the player increases his or her self-doubt. Self-doubt leads to missing putts. As the player misses putts, confidence erodes. His or her feelings of inadequacy further reinforce their basic belief that he or she can't putt. The player may have competence in his or her stroke but is reluctant to trust and believe in it, even though he or she may have the physical tools necessary to putt the ball solidly. If the player doesn't hole putts, confidence erodes and the negative cycle is reinforced.

Some players are so hard on themselves when they miss that they can't see anything positive or give themselves credit for what they did right. They become frustrated and their disappointment breeds feelings of incompetence and a lack of self-trust. The downward spiral continues. The result is a player filled with

The Negative Putting Cycle creats self-doubt and reduces putting confidence.

pessimism and frustration. Negative putters believe they will miss, they think about missing, and they do everything they possibly can to sabotage themselves. However, they are effective in one way; they expect to miss putts and are successful at missing. This cycle repeats and missing becomes an ingrained habit.

Once this vicious cycle gets started, it's hard to break. Players often tell us that they have tried everything possible to get out of their slump, but nothing works. Instead of looking at the real cause, they look at their stroke mechanics or equipment, only to understand that they ultimately must look inside themselves.

FINDING "IT" ON THE GREEN

We always hear of great players, who were once world-class putters, talk about how they used to have "it," but lost "it" over time and years of frustration. They endlessly seek out the perfect stroke or "the golden putter" that will help them replace their lost confidence. They seek gimmicks and band-aid remedies to find the answer to their putting woes. Sometimes band-aids work, but they are usually short-term fixes, and the player must continue searching for a solution.

Great putting and putting confidence begin with the belief that you already "have it." "It" is the power within you to believe in yourself and to accept that you can do whatever you want. "It" is something that is inside you and has always been there. The wonderful thing is that "it" hasn't gone away. "It" never goes away! The only time players lose something is when they convince themselves that they don't have "it."

Most players do not need more instruction, another putter, or critiques of aim and alignment. What they really need is an infusion of their own best medicine—belief in themselves and their putting ability. A touring professional once said, "A player only can endure seeing the ball lip out a certain number of times because the negative pictures provide a backlog of missed opportunities that take their toll on the player's psyche and confidence." The more positive pictures you see, the more positive results you are likely to receive. Confident putters "see" the ball going into the hole. Poor putters "see" the ball lip-out and miss.

You now know that great putters have high levels of self-confidence, but you want to know exactly how to obtain putting confidence. The answer lies ultimately within yourself. You need to find the keys that will unlock your potential for putting success and tap into those keys. However, the search isn't always easy or fruitful. Nor are the results immediate enough for most golfers. But if you are diligent and motivated to improve, the rewards are well-worth the effort. In Chapter 5, we discuss the keys to gaining, improving, and rebuilding your confidence.

Try This!

Think back to when you were putting with high confidence. What were the keys that helped you feel confident, even when you missed putts? What was it like to have total confidence in your putting? What were you feeling? Write down the feelings, thoughts, and emotions you had when putting with high confidence. Use those feelings and thoughts to guide you back on track to elevated feelings of putting confidence. Remember, if you putted well once—you can do it again.

Confidence: The Key to Giving It Your Best Stroke

Confidence develops in many ways, but true confidence comes from establishing a strong foundation for success. Good putters practice in a way that increases their putting competence. They spend time developing their touch on the greens to increase confidence and feel comfortable with their distance control. They do not overload themselves with the latest golf guru's "quick tips." Great putters instill confidence by developing a preshot routine for putting that simplifies their approach to the game. Lastly, great putters develop confidence by committing to the decisions they make on the green.

Everybody likes giving advice to friends. When a good putter misses several putts left of the hole, a playing partner offers advice and says he is "pulling the ball" and needs to change the position of his shoulders to ensure that the putter head moves in a pendulum motion. Most players make a change on the next putt without thinking about what caused the error in the first place. The smart player on the other hand examines the last few putts without changing his or her putting stroke. This allows a player to remain confident in the face of helpful advice from others. LPGA Star Helen Alfredsson said, "I think you need to trust and believe the things that are good for you. When you are not putting well, the tendency is to be looking for or listening to too many things, it gives your mind too many things to process, and sometimes this makes it worse."

How would you react to this situation? Do you have rabbit ears for instructional feedback from your playing partners? Or, do you know what is best for you and how to self-correct your putting? Partners giving instruction may have good intentions, but often they offer information too quickly and it can cause more harm to your game. Be careful about to whom you listen.

COMPETENCE: THE FOUNDATION FOR CONFIDENCE

Great putters develop a solid foundation for putting confidence by generating competence. What is it about your putting method that gives you confidence? Is it your repeating stroke? Is it your ability to hit putts solidly time after time? Is it your ability to gauge distance accurately? Is it your ability to read greens and see the line well? Mastering the physical and mental requirements of putting provides players with a sense of competence or inner comfort, which leads to increased self-confidence on the course.

Confidence follows competence. This means you should practice your putting with the intent to master the skills that lead to competence. The following are some areas that provide a base of support for developing putting confidence.

CONFIDENCE FROM YOUR PRACTICE

Most golfers don't really like to practice putting. In interviews we conducted with the nation's top collegiate golf coaches, their biggest concern was that players didn't practice putting enough or didn't know how to practice the right way. The coaches said that most players would score better if they understood how important putting is and learned good practice habits. Professionals spend at least one to two hours per day on the putting greens. This may not reflect what truly great putters do because they only practice enough to retain feel and reinforce their confidence.

> ## Focusing on what you want to happen helps you approach each putt with a positive action plan.

"If I practice the right way then normally I feel prepared, and then I have confidence."

Vicki Goetze, LPGA Tour

The key is that practice is vital to maintaining and reinforcing your competence. In addition, you must learn to practice with a purpose. Practice to establish feel and touch of the speed of the greens. Practice to master the pendulum motion of the arms and shoulders and to gauge distance through appropriate effort control. Practice to develop an image of the line for breaking putts. Whatever your purpose is, ultimately you need to establish a level of competence in your mental and physical skills that promotes self-confidence on the course.

CONFIDENCE FROM YOUR PREPUTT ROUTINE

Another foundation for confidence is to develop a systematic preputt routine. The purpose of a routine is to lock your mind into the cues that allow you to focus on execution and nothing else (refer to Chapter 7 on preputt routines). Your routine is especially important when you feel the pressure of a "must make" putt. Your routine should help you focus on the task, believe in your method, and trust your decisions, which lead to a smooth and rhythmic stroke. A routine helps you positively lock into your task, no matter what the situation may be. It provides many players with a sense of comfort and trust in their ability, which makes them more self-confident.

CONFIDENCE FROM EXPERIENCE AND COMPETITION

Another foundation for putting competence comes from playing "under the gun" in a competitive golf tournament. Nothing can provide you with a bigger boost of confidence than sinking an important putt during a club championship or going after your best round ever. For players with seriously low putting confidence, golf tournaments become golf "tourniquets," and their putting becomes a bloodletting of serious proportions. A person's perception of the event produces anxiety and low putting confidence makes it even worse.

Many amateur players exaggerate their poor putting in past rounds and let one bad putting round affect their confidence. This is an error in attitude. What happened in the past can only hurt you when you focus on it during the present shot. Refocus on the present putt, and keep your attention on what you want to happen versus what you fear may happen. Use your experience and previous successes, no matter how big or small, to build the foundation for your present putting confidence. Keep in mind that all it takes is one important putt to spark your putting confidence.

> "Every putt you have, you walk up to with the attitude—this is the putt that is going in."
>
> Mike Moraghan, University of Virginia Golf Coach

CONFIDENCE FROM YOUR COMMITMENT

Confidence comes from trusting what you know you can do. Confidence flows from being clear in your mind about what you want to do and committing to that plan. Great putters prepare themselves mentally and physically for every putt. They know the importance of staying committed to their plan and believing that everything they have done to prepare ensures putting success. Jack Nicklaus, Ben Crenshaw, Bob Charles, and Gary Player all talk of the importance of being totally committed to their intended purpose or goal. That purpose is to get the ball into the hole as efficiently as possible.

> "Confidence comes from knowing . . . that I have done it in the past and I can do it again."
>
> Danielle Ammaccapane, LPGA Tour

Putters with less successful results, who have little confidence in their talent, don't always give each putt 100% commitment. Just a hint of self-doubt opens the door for indecision on the green. And indecision is your worst enemy in putting. A mentally disciplined player says, "I'm going to do everything I can to stay committed to my plan."

CONFIDENCE FROM YOUR PREROUND WARM-UP

A practice routine before play helps players gain confidence. Do you step out of the car and walk to the first tee without even testing the speed of the greens? A warm-up is an excellent time to develop a feel for the green. It's a "tune-up" for that day's round. It's not competition, you don't have to win warm-up. Good players use warm-ups only to get a feeling of the ball impacting the putter head and how well the ball is rolling.

As part of their warm-up before going to the first tee, players make a few short putts in a row. This helps them gain confidence by seeing, hearing, and feeling putts fall before going to the first tee. It provides them with a recent "look" of putting success to instill confidence for that day's play. Take advantage of a warm-up by developing feel before walking to the first tee.

CONFIDENCE FROM YOUR PUTTER

Finally, you also can gain confidence from having a putter that looks and feels good. Give a player on tour a week with a putter that feels good and putts start to drop; confidence soars. You will find literally hundreds of putters with various head shapes, weights, lengths, and lofts. Choose a putter that gives you confidence and makes you feel comfortable.

When a player has a putter that suits his or her optical and kinesthetic needs, the player gains comfort and comfort means confidence. Aiming a putter head is an important ingredient in putting. The more comfortable a player feels with his or her alignment, the easier it is to make a determined stroke. When a player has a putter that feels right, he or she usually finds that aim and alignment come easier.

What one player perceives to be heavy and bulky, another may think it feels good and works beautifully. One thing is certain, no matter what putter you use, if you can have success with it, the putter starts to look good. Players develop such trust in a putter that they tend to treasure the putter as if it were magic. Many great players name their magical putters. The most recognizable magic putters are: Ben Crenshaw's "Little Ben," Arnold Palmer's "Old Faithful," Paul Runyan's "Little Poison," and perhaps the most famous putter, Bobby Jones' "Calamity Jane."

Undoubtedly, all great putters have had a hot putter in their hands once, but they all have experienced putting slumps at one time. Many players get a boost from switching putters and using one with a different shape, visual look, or feel. This provides a "newness" and fresh attitude about putting, and for some players this is the spark they need. We don't recommend buying a new putter every time you have a poor putting day. But if you don't feel comfortable with your present putter, you aren't going to feel very confident when it's time to perform. Sometimes a fresh outlook is all you need to change your attitude, and a new putter provides you with a new look. Finally, the putter is not magic. Real magic happens when your hand-eye coordination, attitude, confidence and competence are working toward the same goal: to make a putt.

HOW TO REGAIN CONFIDENCE WHEN YOU'RE LEAKING OIL

Everyone has days when the putts don't fall. Even the best putters in the world struggle on the greens and find it a challenge to maintain and, at times, regain their confidence. If your confidence shatters on the course, this is when you have to intervene and turn it around. Players begin to expect they won't make putts, but it's not certain that you won't make any putts that day. Here are some ideas for regaining confidence when you're leaking oil on the greens.

Only the present putt matters. Too many amateur players lose their confidence when they miss one or two putts early in the round. They talk themselves into thinking that they "can't buy a putt today." The images and results of the last few missed putts fill their mind, and they believe they cannot make the present one.

In reality, only the present putt matters. You need to have the shooter's mentality. Each putt is new, with a different distance, speed, and break. You should approach each putt with a renewed enthusiasm and desire. The past no longer matters, nor should it influence your present putt. If you make putts early, you want to believe you can continue making them. If you miss early, you want to believe the next putt is the one that will get you on a roll.

> "There are times when I thought if I make a putt, it would get the whole round going."
>
> Danielle Ammaccapane, LPGA Tour

Don't let missing affect other parts of your game. When your putting confidence is low, it often can negatively affect other parts of your game, if you let it. You try harder to make up for poor putting and this puts more pressure on other areas of your game. The frustration from lipping-out four times in a row can also spill over into your full shots. And frustration can lead to trying harder to make something happen.

> "If you let a poor putting day work into the rest of your game, then you've got real problems."
>
> Bob Murphy, Senior PGA Tour

You have to be careful not to change your game plan when the putts don't fall. It's easy to press in this situation and try harder to make something happen. Stick to your game plan and don't let negative emotions from putting filter into other shots.

Go back to basics. The best place to start when the wheels fall off is to go back to the basics. Examine the fundamentals of your putting, such as body position, alignment, and the tempo of your stroke. A small adjustment in alignment

---

Missing putts causes frustration and negative thoughts, and causes golfers to search for a "cure."

may greatly affect your comfort level over the ball, and that may be just the spark you need. Don't automatically assume that it's going to be a bad day on the green. Do something active to feel more comfortable and confident when it comes time to stroke the ball.

Stroke it with determination. Realistically, you can't make every putt you look at, but you can think that you will make the present putt. That is how the best putters in the world think. The probability of making a 20-foot putt is lower than the probability of missing, but you still have to think that you will make it. If your confidence is low, stroke the ball with the determination that it is going in the hole. The only other option is to stroke it believing that it will not go in the hole.

> "Accept the fact that you are going to miss some putts, but miss them when trying to make them."
>
> Helen Alfredsson, LPGA Tour

Don't blame yourself. Several extraneous factors, over which you have no control, influence the outcome of a putt. You have to have some good luck to make putts. Spike marks, foot prints, imperfections in the green, an unexpected gust of wind are factors that you cannot control. But they do influence the outcome of a putt.

A player can quickly jump to the conclusion that he or she put a bad stroke on the ball. Maybe it was a spike mark that threw the ball off line. When you blame yourself for missing and think it was something that you did wrong, you destroy your confidence. It's a lot easier to save your confidence when you can chalk up a missed putt to something that is beyond your control.

Mind Matters

When you were younger and learned to ride a bike, what was the most important thing you learned? Probably balance, because you needed it to stay on or you would fall and hurt yourself. Putting is pretty much like riding a bike. You learned it a long time ago and once had positive putting confidence. You weren't afraid of anything. Most of us learn to fear and doubt our putting. You once were a good putter, but now suffer from the putting blues.

Remember, great putting involves saying "I'm confident that I can make putts!" You were once a natural putter, who simply said "Watch this!" You are self-empowered to make the decision that you have control over your putting attitude. You ultimately make the decision about where the ball will break and how much the grain affects the ball's roll. You aim the putter head, align your body on your putting line, and launch the ball with the proper speed and effort control. Accept that you can make putts, and then have confidence that the ball has a good chance of falling into the hole.

Try This!

Here are some ideas to help enhance your confidence. Try these suggestions for two weeks and note any improvements in your putting.

1. Make a mental or physical list of all the times that you felt "confident" during recent playing rounds. List the feelings and thoughts that promote confidence. Notice the ones that occur most often and focus on those particular thoughts and feelings while you prepare for an upcoming round or competition.
2. Develop a preputt routine that is simple, consistent, and helpful when focusing positively on making putts. Overlearn your preputt routine so that it becomes automatic and provides you with stability when you feel anxious or pressured.
3. Incorporate mental discipline into your putting routine and practice sessions. Tell yourself on every putt that you will give 100 percent effort, both physically and mentally.
4. Commit yourself to excellence in reading greens and making clear decisions about where you want to aim and stroke the ball, and then go ahead and do it.
5. Know that putting confidence is a "do it yourself" project that starts from the inside. The more you input positive success pictures, the larger your confidence memory bank.
6. Be mentally tough by shrugging-off missed putts and learning to use selective memory in your putting history. Always focus on the putts that you have made or are making, versus the putts that get away or lip-out.

Line, Speed, and Target: Focus for Making Putts

The ability to focus your mind is critical to successful performance in all sports, especially in golf. During an average round, you spend less than one-half hour actually playing your shots, which leaves more than three hours of downtime. This is a challenge to your concentration because you have to focus in and out constantly. Total concentration is the ability to immerse yourself in a task without becoming distracted. Skilled players like Greg Norman and Seve Ballesteros describe concentration as a state of "flow," being "in a bubble," or "in a cocoon" during which nothing can penetrate their focus.

Dr. Csikszentmihalyi, a psychologist at the University of Chicago, has studied the phenomenon of "flow" throughout his career. He studied basketball players, dancers, rock climbers, chess players, factory workers and others to understand why people enjoy activities even when there are no inherent rewards. He found that when people become fully absorbed in an activity, they reach a state of flow.

Four elements must be present to get into the flow state: (1) the presence of a challenging activity; (2) the skills match the challenge; (3) the presence of clear goals; and (4) the availability of instant feedback about how you are doing.

When these elements are present, Dr. "C" says an "order in consciousness" occurs. This phenomenon is what helps people become immersed in an activity and have fun. The exciting finding is that anyone can reach a flow state. We certainly know that all four elements are present in putting. Putting is challenging and most people possess the skills required to make putts. The goal is clear, and you get instant feedback—you either make or miss the putt.

Have you ever said to yourself, "I just didn't concentrate well for that shot?" If so, then you know how hard it is to focus your mind for an extended period of time without becoming distracted. Most players, at one time, have blanked-out, become distracted, or become too tired to concentrate. Even the greatest players in the world have trouble concentrating when they are bored or anxious. In the pages to follow, we discuss concentration and its enemies. Later, we discuss specific methods for improving your focus on the course.

UNDERSTANDING CONCENTRATION

You see two basic styles of concentration in golf. Some players, like Ben Hogan, focus intensely for the entire round. This demands the ability to maintain concentration for extended periods. Other players, like Lee Trevino, prefer to focus only for the shot and then relax their concentration between shots. You may have a preferred style, but to hit your best shot, you must totally focus on execution when it's your turn to play.

Good concentration involves several elements. These include (1) knowing what cues to focus on; (2) staying focused on those relevant cues; (3) keeping a narrow and external focus; (4) shifting attention; (5) knowing how to refocus when distracted; and (6) controlling your thoughts.

What Are the Important Cues?

From the time you read how a putt breaks to the time you strike the ball, you must learn to focus only on important cues and disregard all irrelevant cues. Since speed and direction are the two most important elements in putting, you must focus on cues that help you plan for the speed and direction of the putt. You must evaluate the type of grass on the green, the slope of the green, the direction of the grain of the grass, the moisture on the green, the wind, and any experiences you have had on that particular green. Attention then shifts to execution. You follow your normal routine by taking practice strokes, aligning to the target, looking at your spot/target, and using a swing cue to initiate your stroke. These are the performance cues that help you make the putt. It sounds simple, but we all know that focusing on those cues is easier said than done.

What Is Relevant and Irrelevant to Putting?

To putt well, you have to read the green, make a decision on the break and speed, and go through your routine without interruption or distraction. Problems start when distractions and other mental detours sidetrack you from your objective. Most destroyers of attention are self-induced, such as fear, doubt, and worry. You can deal with idle chatter while putting, but it's hard to stop thinking about three-putting once the thought comes to mind.

The first step is to know the important cues for reading greens (refer to Chapter 7 on Vision and Imagination in Putting) and the elements of your routine that help you putt well. When you have a routine, it becomes a matter of keeping your mind locked into the relevant cues without doubting your read, tensing up over the ball, or letting negative thoughts pull you off the task.

> "You need to focus on something, and what is more natural to focus on than the ball and the hole?"
>
> Helen Alfredsson, LPGA Tour

Don't Reflect, React

In any sport, athletes reach peak performance when they focus intensely on the task and react automatically to the situation. But putting doesn't require reaction to a dynamic action like batting in baseball or spiking in volleyball, yet peak performance occurs when you let it happen. A batter doesn't have time to think after the pitcher releases the ball; he must react. It takes about 0.4 seconds for the ball to arrive at the plate. The batter uses about 0.2 seconds to recognize the pitch and 0.2 seconds to decide to swing and then move the bat to meet the ball. Thus, the batter must rely on his experience and instinct to hit the ball. When he thinks about what to do, it's too late, the ball is past him.

> **Overanalyzing and thinking too much during the stroke can paralyze or "freeze" the golfer.**

Too many players paralyze themselves by overanalyzing or thinking too much on the putting green. They paralyze themselves by thinking too much about their stroke, what their instructor said, or they worry about making or missing. Like the batter, an external and narrow focus is best because it allows you to react to what you see. When you focus internally, you become too mechanical or fixated on yourself. You perform at your peak when you keep an external-narrow task focus, like a tennis player does when watching a moving tennis ball. You have to simplify your approach to putting. The first things you must do is stop giving yourself verbal instructions, forget about mechanics, and let your experience and instinct take over.

Focus on Execution, Not Result

Most great putters focus on execution and the task of rolling their ball on line. They know they can make putts, but they don't try to make putts. Focusing on the result of missing or making is not a priority. If they complete their task correctly, the putts will fall. Great putters focus on the task of selecting and hitting their line. If you select the correct line and can roll the ball along your line, you have done your task. What happens after that is out of your control. Even if you didn't make the putt, if you hit the line you selected, you were successful. Sometimes you can do everything right and still miss.

> "I don't try to make a putt, I just try to get the ball rolling on my line."
>
> Greg Kraft, PGA Tour

Focus In and Focus Out

The stop and go action in golf demands a special kind of ability that other continuous tasks like running or swimming don't require. During play, you

> **Total focus means forgetting the past and staying in the present.**

focus intensely for 30–40 seconds to play a shot and then have a few minutes before your next shot. It's hard for many players to refocus after a long lapse in play. Have you ever felt out of sync or lost your rhythm when you had to wait for the group ahead of you? If you did, you probably had difficulty fully refocusing your mind when it was your turn to play.

Getting Back on Track

Concentration also involves the ability to refocus after distractions. It doesn't help to be thinking about the last putt you missed when you're playing the present shot. The key is to be able to refocus and pull your mind back to the task. You first must be aware that you're not focused and then you may adjust your focus or stop to refocus your mind.

> "You have to be able to override distractions and focus on the right area."
>
> Cindy Schreyer, LPGA Tour

Stop the Wandering

We think that concentration ultimately involves the ability to control your thoughts. If you can control what you are thinking about, you can control your concentration. A player who can't focus on the present hurts his or her chances of making putts. If you think ahead to the next tee shot or about how mad you are about three-putting the last hole while you're trying to make a putt, your mind is wandering from your immediate task. You must learn to program your mind like a computer. You get ahead of yourself when you think about the result, missing, or making a birdie putt. You must have the discipline to run the program that you choose, rather than let your mind deviate from its goal.

ATTENTION KILLERS

How do you typically lose your focus? Think about the last few rounds you played. Is there a pattern to how or when you lost your focus? Here are some problems with concentration that you might recognize.

Outside Distractions

Players are distracted by noises or visual distractions. Some tour players are so sensitive to sound that they become distracted by clubs rattling in a player's bag on the adjacent fairway. A player who is sensitive to visual disturbances can spot someone walking as far away as 50 feet with his peripheral vision.

The Blank Out

Many golfers have experienced the "I wasn't focusing on anything" syndrome. If you blank out, you realize what happened, but only after you hit the shot. It's too late to stop a "no-brain" shot after it is over. If you go braindead, it can ruin your putting performance. That is why it is important to have a routine that you can follow so you know what to think about and focus on when putting (refer to Chapter 8 on developing a preputt routine).

Negative Thoughts

Negative thoughts can ruin your ability to focus on the task. Thoughts of missing, three-putting, or losing the match create negative images, which program you for failure. It's a negative spiral. When you miss, you think more about missing. When you think about missing, you miss more. But there is hope. You can learn to reprogram yourself with positive thoughts and images by first learning to recognize when your mind gets caught in a negative spiral, and then replacing a negative thought with a positive one.

"I don't think good putters ever think what they are putting for."

Puggy Blackmon, University of South Carolina Golf Coach

Anxiety

Anxiety and fear are the biggest killers of attention. It's hard to focus on execution when you are afraid of three-putting. Anxiety usually results from thinking about negative consequences or missing, which threatens your ego. Anxiety increases physical tension, which further distracts you from your goal. When you become anxious, you lose some performance cues because your perceptual field shrinks. This causes you to disregard important information needed to putt well. For example, you may become fixated on the line of your putt when anxious, and then forget the speed and leave the putt a foot short.

Boredom

Your attention also suffers when you are bored. If you're not challenged, you become bored and lose interest. A lack of challenge takes you below your optimal level of activation or excitement. In this state, your focus is too broad (you take in too much irrelevant information), and you lose the pinpoint focus needed to putt well. Your mind wanders back and forth to irrelevant cues that have nothing to do with execution.

Low Self-Confidence

Low self-confidence is another attention killer. When you attempt to sink a putt, what do you need to help you focus on making the putt? Self-confidence for sure. If you don't think you can make a putt, you become anxious and think "just get it close" or "don't three-putt". Since a person with low confidence is afraid of missing, it's hard to focus on execution. As your confidence increases, your anxiety and fear of missing decrease.

Running Out of Steam

A player who attempts to concentrate for the entire round may have trouble concentrating during the last few holes. For some players, mental energy can be finite. By the 15th or 16th holes, these players start to lose focus and blank out over shots. If you have trouble concentrating for the last few holes, we recommend that you relax your concentration between holes and save it so you don't run out of steam. When it is time for you to play your shot, you can then tune your focus back in.

OFF-COURSE EXERCISES TO IMPROVE YOUR FOCUS

You can use several strategies to improve your focus on the greens. One way is to practice improving your concentration off the course so you can focus better on the course. There also are many techniques you can use on the green to keep your mind locked into the task.

Exercise 1: Holding Your Focus

A simple exercise you can do to test your concentration ability is to look at an object like a golf ball and keep your focus on it without letting other thoughts come to mind. Examine the ball in full detail. Look at the dimples, the writing, the size and color, and feel the weight of the ball in your hand. See how long you can keep your attention on the ball without becoming distracted by another thought. Just start with one full minute and progress to five minutes.

Exercise 2: Focusing on Breathing

This is a simple exercise that you can do any time to improve your ability to lock your mind into one thought. Sitting or lying down, focus all your energy on your breathing. Smooth out your breathing, count to six as you inhale and six as you exhale. Focus completely on the rhythm of your breathing. Feel the air going in and out of your lungs. See how long you can focus on your breathing before you become distracted by another thought. If another thought comes to mind, let it pass and get back to your breathing exercise. Practice this exercise for 10 minutes a day until you can totally focus on breathing.

Exercise 3: Mental Rehearsal

An excellent exercise to help improve concentration and program the mind and body with positive images is mental practice. This exercise requires you to recall past images and feelings in a systematic fashion. In your mind's eye, recall a familiar golf course. Your task is to play the course in your mind, shot by shot, until you begin to lose your focus or become distracted. This helps you control your thoughts and images and focus on playing well.

Start on the first tee. Recall in as much detail as you can the terrain of the course, grass, trees, lakes, smells, feelings, and any other images that you associate with that hole. Experience yourself playing your first shot in as much detail as possible and then walk to your next shot. Play as many holes as you can until you lose focus. If you can play two holes without losing focus, try for three holes the next time. Just keep increasing the length of time you can hold your focus.

Exercise 4: Practice Refocusing Attention

First, make one column on a blank piece of paper and list the circumstances in which you lose focus, and in the next column write down what happens to your focus. For example, "I lose my focus when others are watching me try to make a short putt." What happens is: "I begin to think about how stupid I would look if I missed it." Once you create a list, you have a better idea of your limitations and can then mentally practice refocusing your attention for each of these situations.

In the previous example, imagine yourself in that same situation. You are standing over a short putt and you start to think about looking stupid if you miss it. Say "stop" to yourself and imagine pulling your mind back to the line and speed of the putt and think about execution. Do this with each situation you listed. Then, when it happens the next time you play, you will know how to deal with it.

ON-COURSE TIPS FOR BETTER CONCENTRATION

No Past, No Future, Only the Present

Remember to stay focused in the present on the requirements of the task. A big error that players make is thinking ahead about the results of making or missing a putt, or thinking about the last putt they missed. You first have to be aware that you are not focused, and then pull your attention back to the present. Stay focused on execution in the present moment.

Think One Shot at a Time

"Play one shot at a time" is a phrase that we use a lot in our work with golfers, and it can't be used enough. Your performance suffers when you are thinking about the 220-yard drive you must hit to carry the pond on the last hole when you are hitting your putt on the 10th. And you can't be thinking about the last putt you missed as you stand over your present putt. To help stay focused in the present, think about playing only that one shot. Separate that one shot from the rest and look at it as a game in itself.

Focus on Your Preparation

You should know your specific routine you use to prepare to putt. A routine fills your mind with only positive cues. If you don't have a routine, your mind will wander aimlessly while you prepare to hit your putt. Your routine should help you analyze the variables that influence the line and speed of the putt, set-up to the target, and execute your stroke. If you have trouble focusing on any of these tasks, it's time for you to develop a personal preshot routine.

Relax While You Wait Your Turn

You should be ready to play when it is your turn to putt, but you don't want to overanalyze and overread your putt. You also don't want to tax your concentration before you putt. Once you look at the break of the putt, relax your focus and "save" it for your putt. Focusing intensely on your putt while you wait stresses your ability to concentrate when it's time to play.

Use a Warm-Up Routine

All good players have a warm-up ritual they follow before tee-off to help them get focused for play. Most tour players start their warm-up on the practice tee after doing stretching exercises. They hit short irons and swing easy to warm up their muscles for action. They might hit five balls with each designated club. Then, they warm up on the green to get a feel for the speed of the green. Finally, they may finish hitting some chip shots or bunker shots. A warm-up routine allows players to get their mind focused on the match, similar to a runner who has a stretching routine before he or she runs, or a pilot who runs through a checklist before take-off.

Practice Like You Play

Do you practice with a mission? Or do you hit 30 putts from the same spot and continue raking in new balls without changing your alignment or target? How often do you hit 30 putts from the same position on the golf course? Many players make the mistake of practicing in a way that doesn't help their performance on the golf course. Each time you hit a putt on the golf course, it has a different speed, length, and visual look. Practice your putting like you play on the golf course. Play 18 holes on the practice green. Use your regular preputt routine. Hit different putts from different distances and various breaking putts each time. Challenge yourself to break par on the practice green. This type of practice is more specific to what you encounter during actual play.

Cue Yourself to Concentrate

If you are the last to putt, sometimes it's hard to refocus your mind when it's your turn to play. And in some cases you may wait for longer than five or six minutes. You must then fully concentrate once it is your turn to play. To do this, use a physical trigger, such as placing your ball on your ball mark as a cue to start focusing. At this point you want to turn your attention to preparation and execution for the putt, and if anything else enters your mind, let it pass through your mind.

Rehearse Your Putt while You Wait

If you have trouble refocusing after a long delay and it's your turn to putt, try rehearsing your putt. Imagine the line of the putt given what you have seen thus far. Physically take a couple practice swings and then "see" the ball rolling along your line into the hole. When it is your turn to play, it will be second nature for you.

Try This!

The next time you are on the putting green, ask a friend to distract you while you putt. Go through your entire routine and see if you can focus intensely on your routine while someone tries to distract you. Don't try to block out the distraction. Instead, focus intensely on your routine and execution. The better you can focus during this exercise, the better you become at dealing with distractions on the course.

Now You See It: Vision and Imagination in Putting

Good vision and using your eyes to gain reliable information are important to good putting. You must learn to read greens well, see your line clearly, and trust what you see before you stroke the ball. You can see the intense focus in the eyes of a player who is concentrating well, such as Jack Nicklaus' intense stare on the green. Raymond Floyd also has the "icy stare" on the putting green. What is it about the look of these great players? A consensus among other golf pros rate Nicklaus and Floyd as two of the best all-time clutch putters, if not general putters. They have great vision and use it to evaluate how a putt will react on the green. They also are good at using their imagination to plan a course of action.

> "You feel a golf course with your eyes. You play golf with your eyes. People just don't realize this. Your eyes tell you everything about the wind, the greens, everything."
>
> Gary Player (Peper, 1988), Senior PGA Tour

DIFFERENCES IN VISION BETWEEN GREAT AND POOR PUTTERS

Do great putters have better eyesight than average players? Do great putters read greens differently or more accurately than poor putters? Many people believe that professional golfers on the PGA, Senior PGA, and LPGA tours have better vision and visual skills compared to normal golfers. It may be true that professionals visualize more clearly and obtain more reliable information on greens than the average players. This may be due to the enormous amount of time they spend perfecting their putting over different surfaces and grasses. Research has shown that many tour players have very good vision. Some have superior visual skills and visual acuity (sharpness of sight), yet some have less than perfect vision, and have overcome that impediment through hard work and perseverance.

Most notable are former U.S. Open Champions Tom Kite and Hale Irwin. Both Kite and Irwin were tested without prescription lenses at 20/400 (they see at 20 feet what most people see at 400 feet), but with corrective glasses or contacts, their vision is 20/20. Superior vision doesn't guarantee putting success, but vision plays a crucial role in helping you make putts.

Great putters gather more accurate information than poor putters. Great putters also trust what they see better than do average putters. They are more decisive and can easily shed self-doubt and indecision. They imagine positive outcomes. Poor putters don't know how to gather usable information. They are unsure of what they see and search for too many cues, which can lead to information overload. Poor putters also doubt how they read the putt and how much the ball breaks and how many breaks they see. They wonder if their body and putter are aligned correctly. Poor putters don't know if they can launch the ball on line or if they can stroke putts the right distance. Little wonder, with all this uncertainty, why they putt poorly.

VISION AND YOUR PUTTING ROUTINE

How often have you seen players rush putts only to miss in frustration? They do not take time to evaluate and assess their putt. They rush up to the ball without reading the putt or making a decision about the line. Poor putters don't have a routine that helps them accurately assess their putts. A routine guides a player through their preparation by helping him or her read putts, visualize the break, align consistently to the target, and stroke the ball with confidence. Seeing the right cues does not guarantee success on the putting green, but it is an important first step to great putting.

SURVEYING THE GREEN: GETTING A READ

You may have a smooth putting stroke and a great attitude but if you can't read greens accurately, you have little chance of ever becoming a great putter. The good news is that reading greens is a skill you can improve. Once you know how to read greens, your competence level increases and so does your putting confidence.

You have to know how to assess a green in order to read it accurately. Most players' feelings of helplessness come from not knowing how to judge how a ball reacts on the green. Assessing the green provides you with needed information to help you plan a putting strategy. You have to know where you want to hit a putt before you can play your shot.

Reading greens starts when you approach the green and survey the lay of the green. Today's golf architects do a terrific job of designing greens. Your job is to understand the contour of the green and how it will affect your putt. This is the first challenge of great putting. What is the general shape of the green? Is it round, kidney shaped, or irregular? Next, you want to look for the lay of the earth on which the green sits. If you play on elevated greens, they may have built-in undulations and raised contours. If the greens are flat, then perhaps they are older greens and may have hidden raised spots or crowns which have evolved through years of maturation.

Is there any trouble? Sand traps and water hazards are placed strategically close to low areas. Errant putts can get dangerously close to the water's edge on today's penalty course designs. Also, when sand traps and bunkers are located next to greens, sand and dirt pile up in that area over the years. Eventually, the green slopes away from the trap and a small hill grows out of the side near the trap, which slants toward the middle of the green.

"Don't make your stroke until you have the best read you can get."

Greg Norman (1988), PGA Tour

Look at Putt from All Angles

Obtaining the correct information helps you make good decisions.

Also, observe if the green slopes from back to front or vice versa. Does it have dips, hills, or multiple levels built into it? Where is the highest point on the green? Knowing that, you will have a very good idea of which way the putt will break. Sometimes, architects try to fool you with mounds. Knowing how and where the ball will break off these artificial undulations makes reading the putt easier.

WATCH OTHER PUTTS: YOUR BEST CLUE

You can learn a lot about a green by just watching other players' shots, especially short chips and longer putts. Other players' putts allow you "go to school" on the roll of the ball, which helps you understand the break and speed of the green. Take advantage of what you see happen on the green, it will save you strokes. You can also learn clues from your first putt and how it reacts around the hole. Watch carefully if it passes the hole so you will know how to play your second putt.

You must consider several other factors when reading greens. Fast greens will have more break given the same slope angle. Drier greens are generally faster than wet greens. Wet greens do not break as much as dry greens, and are slower due to the moisture holding the ball on line. The grain of the green—how the grass lays on the green—also affects your putt. When you putt with the grain, the ball travels farther than if you hit a putt against the grass grain. The grain can also help a putt break more or hold the putt on line depending on the direction of the grain. Strong winds influence your putt especially on faster greens. Look for these cues on the greens to help you better understand how a ball will react on the green.

THE DOMINANT EYE IN PUTTING

Our work and research shows that your dominant eye is important to successful putting. We studied the effects of the dominant eye in people's ability to aim at a target, and how vision and aiming relate to confidence. Most players were just as confident when aligning themselves with only the dominant eye compared to using both eyes. Yet, these players did not feel as confident when they aligned to a target with their non-dominant eye. Using the dominant eye to sight putts does provide a feeling of confidence.

Your dominant eye is important for alignment because the dominant eye gives you the most accurate information. The notion that it doesn't matter which eye you use for sighting a target is false. It makes good sense to use the directional or dominant eye to align yourself and your putter head to the target.

What is the best way to sight your target? Should you use both eyes when you line-up a putt and when you are over the ball? Yes, you obtain better information with binocular vision (both eyes). Binocular vision is necessary for three-dimensional viewing. It gives you figure-ground relationships, visual balance, depth perception, and distance judgment. These are necessary components to gaining "touch".

One problem occurs with binocular vision though. When standing over a putt, some players tilt their head in a way that causes their eyes to be out of alignment with their line. When you turn your eyes toward the putting cup with the head rotating off the putting line, your visual system is disoriented. You should keep both of your eyes on your line and directed toward your target or spot by turning your head and eyes on this line. This provides you with the most accurate system for maintaining your read and target awareness. Most importantly, keep your dominant eye focused on your line or target when turning your head.

THE MILLION-DOLLAR LOOK

How often do you view your putt from behind the ball, address the ball, and then see a different line and change your target? You probably said, "Why did I change my mind? If I putted to my original spot, I would have made it." The answer is simple. When you move from behind the ball to over the ball, your perception changed due to the changes in your viewing angle. This is known as the visual parallax effect. It's easy to see a different line because your eyes are no longer behind the ball on the putting line. Your eyes are now above the line. When you see two lines, this only creates self-doubt and indecision, which leads to tentative putting.

> **The Million-Dollar Look gives you the best view of the correct line. Don't change your mind once you are over the ball.**

Great putters use their eyes to provide them with information about the green, line, grain, break, and distance, but they use the most accurate information available to them. Golfers squat down behind the ball on the putting line to gain more reliable information. Viewing the putt with your eyes looking down the line (binocular vision) provides visual cues for accurate line detection and depth perception. This allows a player to see the undulations and breaks of the green more accurately than from the address position.

> "Never hit a putt until you have a good vision of the path on which it will roll."
>
> Greg Norman (1988), PGA Tour

Sports vision experts say that you use binocular vision on a horizontal plane when you squat down behind the ball on your putting line. When you stand over a putt at the address position, the way we use our eyes changes into a parallax or vertical plane. Sighting a putt from a vertical plane makes it hard to see the line. The visual cues at address position are less reliable than when your eyes are behind the ball, close to the ground.

The Million-Dollar Look is your best viewing angle for making a decision on what the putt will do. You have to force yourself to keep a fresh image in mind as you move to address the ball. You must stay committed to your target and not give in to a "cheaper," less trustworthy look when over the ball. Doing these things helps you stroke the ball with determination. You may not make a million, but it simplifies your putting and helps you reduce doubt.

DEVELOPING AN EYE FOR THE LINE

Your eyes provide information that you send to your brain for planning, strategy, and decision making. Your eyes dictate your judgment of distance and eventually the effort needed to impact the ball. Speed is the most important element in putting because speed determines the line you select. A player who can judge distance and control speed has good feel and touch. You have several options for making a five-foot putt with a slight break left to right. You can hit it firm and play no break. Or, you can play the putt at the left side of the hole with some break and hit it softer. Lastly, you can start the ball outside the hole and hit it so it dies into the left side of the cup.

> "Seeing the lines and reading greens is really high on the list, it's almost as important as speed and preshot routine."
>
> Bob Burns, PGA Tour

These strategies differ in the way the golfer views them or needs to putt according to how he sees the putt in his mind's eye. How you putt changes depending on your style and the conditions. A confident player may want to take out the break and hit it firm. But if the putt is fast and downhill, you may need another approach. The type of putt you have and your confidence level determines how you imagine the putt in your mind's eye. The next step is to program your body with positive images. Once you select a line with given speed, ingrain that image by repeatedly imagining the ball traveling along your line with the correct speed.

THE BIG PICTURE: SOFT FOCUS OR HARD FOCUS?

Many players become intimidated when they face a long putt. They fear the prospect of three-putting. On longer putts, it is better to concentrate on distance rather than direction. Most three-putts result from knocking the ball past the hole and having a return putt of four, five or even 10 feet. The solution lies in your planning. Using a combination of soft focus and hard focus helps you plan for the putt.

A "soft focus" allows you to see the total distance the putt must travel to get to the hole. It gives you a sense of how far away the hole is and orients you to where it is. Also, it allows you to focus "softly" on the line over the entire distance, which helps lock in the feeling for how hard you must hit the putt.

You use a "hard focus" to see the exact spot on the green that you want to "launch" the ball. This spot could be a line on the green or the final break point on the green. The break point is a spot the ball must go over to take the break to go in the hole. You also use a hard focus for sensing how the ball reacts the last three feet of the putt. The ball is moving the slowest and breaks more when closer to the hole.

Thus, your vision goes from broad (soft focus) to narrow (hard focus) as you prepare for the putt. This allows you to scan the overall picture and then "fine tune" your vision to specific details. This strategy helps funnel your attention. You start out wide with a complete picture of your putt, and narrow it down to a specific target focus.

FOCUS ON A SMALL TARGET

When faced with a long putt, many golf instructors advise players to putt to an imaginary circle around the hole about three feet in diameter. This concept allows a comfortable margin of error and "frees" the player to make a solid stroke and if not successful, the player hopefully has a tap-in. However, the large circle concept may not be precise enough for accurate focus. We think that this method is not specific enough. Looking at a smaller or more specific target increases the chances of getting the ball close to your target.

Throwing darts is an excellent example of this concept. If you try to make a bullseye by looking at the entire board, you won't be successful. If you focus on the bulls-eye, you are becoming more precise with your visual aim. The target is smaller and your focus becomes more intense. The more exact and precise your aim, the more precise information you provide your body. Remember that where your eyes focus—the mind and body follows.

A specific focus is equally effective on short putts. Select a small target located somewhere on your line or near the hole. Pick out a discoloration, ball mark, or spot on your line to aim for. If you are looking inside the cup, find a spot inside the cup toward which you want to aim. Either method works, just make sure that you commit to that spot or line, and aim and fire away.

> "Focus on a narrow target, like a blade of grass, if you miss it, you won't be that far off target."
>
> Vicki Goetze, LPGA Tour

ARE YOU REALLY SQUARE?

An important visual element in putting is aiming the putter where you want the ball to go. Many golfers blame poor putting on their stroke, their putter, the greens, and everything but the real culprit: faulty aim. Knowing that you aim properly at your intended target provides you with confidence that transfers to your putting stroke. If you don't feel comfortable with your aim, it's hard to make a good stroke. You should aim your putter head 90 degrees or perpendicular to your putting line.

The problem is that most people don't aim properly. The reason is that most people don't know what a "square" putter face looks like. Most players set the putter behind the ball, align themselves, and think the putter is square when it really is not. They play with an altered position and ingrain this "look" to the point where they have deceived themselves into believing it is square. What many players think was a pull or a push, may be a perfect stroke.

If poor aiming causes poor set-up, you need to compensate with your stroke to square the putter face at impact. Great putters have a consistent system for getting the putter face square at impact. You must believe that you are aimed correctly. This feeling helps you stroke the ball with determination. Find a method to consistently aim your putter and align your body to your target. This at least gives you the feeling of proper alignment.

VISUAL SHIFT AND IMAGE DECAY DURING PUTTING

Visual shift is a process that occurs during putting, as you look back and forth at the ball and the hole. You have a short recovery period just after the visual shift, during which your vision needs time to refocus on the new object. This is known as accommodation. The faster a player's visual recovery from a far to near object, the better the chance he or she has of retaining a strong target image. Research on tour players' eyes reveal that the better putters have a quicker accommodation time than poor putters. This tells us that the ability to refocus your sight rapidly is a key to good putting. The best focus shift is about one second for good putters.

Putting requires you to focus on a specific target. After imprinting the target in your mind's eye, your sight shifts back to refocus on the ball. The image of the target or line in your mind's eye decays rapidly (within about two seconds). The more time you spend over the ball, the easier it is to lose the image and feel of your target. Staring at the ball for several seconds causes a visual decay of the image of the target. Also, standing over the putt too long invites doubt, which creates tension. Thus, putting without delay after you refocus on the ball helps you keep a strong ball-target orientation and combat self-doubt.

KEEP PUTTING SIMPLE

The visual system is the most dominant sensory system in the body. You transmit at least 80 percent of all information to the brain via your visual system. In a sense, where the visual system goes, your mind and body follows. Where do you focus your vision when putting? Are you looking at specific spots where you want the ball to travel? Or, do you see places that you try to avoid? Do you see the ball go into the hole before you stroke it? Or are you seeing the ball lip-out? Do you use your eyes to give you positive information for your upcoming putt?

> "The simpler you keep your swing and thinking, the better off you will be."
>
> Hubert Green (1994), PGA Tour

What you see is what you get. Putting is truly a visual task. You use your eyes from start to finish. Putting can and should be simple. The key is to use your eyes to gain accurate information and improve your chances of success on the putting green.

Try These Exercises for Improving Vision!

Exercise 1.

The next time you practice, shift your vision from the hole to the ball and try to refocus on the ball as quickly as possible, and then pull the putter back without delay. When you speed up the initiation of your stroke, your speed, distance judgement, and direction improve immediately.

Try an exercise at home to increase eye flexibility and improve accommodation. This is suggested by Dr. Herbert Price of the Sports Vision Center of Indiana. It's called the "Visual Push-Up" and helps train and strengthen the eye muscles responsible for accommodation. Hold your index finger out in front of your eyes a distance of 12 inches. Focus in on your fingerprint or nail for two seconds. Now look across the room and focus in on an object about 10 or 15 feet away. Focus in on that object for about two seconds and then switch back to your index finger. Shift your vision back and forth for 10 minutes a day during your daily schedule.

Exercise 2.

Turn your head to the left, as if you are looking at a putting cup (if left-handed, look right), look at something close to the ground, about ten feet away and maintain focus on it for about two seconds. Now, shut your eyes. What do you see? If you sighted an object, it will appear in a grayish or colored form in your mind's eye. Now, look at it again. Examine the target for five seconds. Now, shut your eyes. With your index finger of your left hand, point to the center of the object without looking at it. How accurately could you point to your spot? Are you off to the left or right? This is called spacial localization, which tests your awareness of the position of objects according to your position in space. Try this exercise on the putting green. Try to obtain a fix on your target and retain an image of the target in your mind's eye. This helps you know exactly where the cup is located, which is important in putting.

Exercise 3.

What does a square putter face look like visually behind the ball? Place black electrical tape on a straight edge or line, and extend the line out five feet or so. At the end of the line, place another line of about six inches across the top so that you form a small "T". Place your putter head on that small "T" and set the putter face square to the small line. The putter head will now be perpendicular to the other black line. A perfectly square 90-degree angle could be measured from the putter head to that line. Now, look down at the putter head in this position. Does it look different from before? If it does, then this will tell you that your optics were off. Looking down the putter head with a visual reference will reinforce the look of square.

The 30-Second Mindset: Establishing a Putting Routine

An important behavior for any player is a preshot routine for putting. A preshot routine helps create a scoring attitude by increasing confidence, focus, and trust. Such a routine is a set of behaviors, both mental and physical, which allow you to prepare your mind and body for successful execution. A routine is the software package that drives your performance. If you don't have a strategy that helps you approach each putt with confidence, focus, and composure, then read the following pages carefully.

WHAT'S ALL THE FUSS ABOUT A PRESHOT ROUTINE?

A routine has many useful purposes. First, it's a tool to help you focus on the task. Without a routine, your mind is free to wander aimlessly to irrelevant details. A routine is also excellent for deflecting pressure. Pressure throws off your rhythm when you let it affect you. Perceived pressure leads to anxiety and tension, which causes you to think ahead about the possible results of your putt. Immersing yourself in your routine helps to keep your mind in the present and on positive thoughts. Greg Norman (1988) says that a routine "keeps your mind off negative thoughts and establishes a rhythm for the entire stroke."

A prestroke routine also builds tempo for a shot. The rhythm or flow of a routine carries you into your putting stroke. Lastly, a routine builds confidence and helps you play more instinctively. With a routine, you are free to putt boldly with confidence and determination. It's harder to be mechanical with your stroke when you trust and have faith in your decisions and plan.

TAKE IT FROM THE PROS

Athletes from several sports use routines. Basketball players use a preshot routine at the foul line. They bounce the basketball a few times and twirl the ball the same way on each free throw. Baseball players use a systematic routine for settling into the batter's box to prepare themselves for a pitch. After each pitch, they step out of the batter's box and engage their routine. Bowlers approach a frame the same way every time. Their behaviors are consistent for each shot, from drying their hands to setting up for a shot, to the number of steps they take during the throw. When you watch tour golfers, you can see that each of them has a defined routine for putting. Some players' routines are more elaborate than others, and each player adopts his or her own style, but each player's routine is consistent.

We think there are three fundamental objectives to a preshot routine for putting. The primary objective is to feel confident. If you lack confidence to make the putt, most likely you will miss. The elements of a good routine should help you eliminate all doubt and indecision and free yourself to make a good stroke.

The next objective is to be immersed in the task. To putt well, you have to keep your mind totally focused in the present moment. You don't want your mind to wander and think about the difficulty of the three holes you have yet to play. The final objective of a routine is to be instinctive and reflexive while executing the stroke. The biggest cause of poor execution is the tendency to consciously control the putter and steer the ball on line. A well-grooved stroke should not be consciously controlled. A good routine allows you to be automatic and trust your stroke.

THE SIX ESSENTIALS: QUALITIES OF A GOOD ROUTINE

A preshot routine has several different steps and each person's routine varies from the next. Depending on the player, a routine may have as many as 15 personalized behaviors, which is too complicated to discuss for our purposes. For simplification, we outline six essential behaviors of a good routine. From these six ingredients, you can develop a personal routine that complements your playing style and personality.

Specific intention. You have to start with a plan—a plan consisting of where and how you want to putt the ball. Your first step is to assess the speed, slope, and terrain of the green. As discussed earlier, your ability to read the putt and make a final decision is critical. You don't want to send vague information to your body. It's important to pick a specific target. This means choosing the line and speed of the putt. If you don't know how it will react, it's still better to make an educated guess. Make up your mind before you step up to the ball.

Mental blueprint. Once you have a specific plan, it's time to program yourself with a mental blueprint. A mental blueprint is a visual image, a sensation, an intuition, or a feeling of how the putt will react on the green. For most players, a mental blueprint is an image of the line of the putt, a visual image of the ball rolling along its line, or simply a feeling of how much the ball will break, if any, on the green. A blueprint is a vital part of programming yourself because it sends specific signals to your body about your plan.

Most visual players see a line from their ball to the hole and imagine their ball rolling along the hole. The mental blueprint gives your body something specific to which to respond. Without a blueprint, you can't execute a good shot.

Physical and mental rehearsal. The third ingredient of a routine is taking a practice run of the stroke you intend to use to carry out your plan. A rehearsal stroke should mirror your actual stroke of the present putt. The rehearsal

A mental blueprint helps you to program exactly what you want to make happen.

stroke is another way of physically programming your body. It helps warm up your muscles and capture the feeling of the tempo of the stroke needed to carry out your plan. It's also a trial run for your plan and mental blueprint. If the tempo of your practice stroke doesn't match your blueprint, then you need to adjust.

Accurate aim and alignment. Aiming and aligning to your intended line is critical to successful putting. Without correct aim or alignment, it doesn't matter how confident you are; you won't make many putts (refer to Chapter 7 on Vision and Putting). If you are aligned wrong, you then must compensate with your putting stroke. For example, if you align to the right of your target, you must pull the putter across your body to start the ball on line. Aiming is also critical because it guides your alignment. If you can't aim your putter and body on your putting line, your alignment will be incorrect. The key is to find a systematic procedure for aiming your putter and aligning yourself to the target. When your aim is set, you want to feel comfortable with it and be able to fire away without hesitation.

Continuous movement. A good routine should flow from start to finish. Periods of inactivity in a routine invite doubt, indecision, and hesitation. These feelings prevent you from making a smooth and relaxed putting stroke. The longer you hesitate, the more time you allow to doubt your decision. Most players' routines flow well until just before they pull the trigger. Just before they stroke the putt, they hesitate as though they are waiting to feel ready. Mechanical players take more time because they have a 10-item checklist before they can start the putter back, and the longer they wait, the more time they have to be mechanical with the stroke and doubt their ability to make the putt.

> "The less time you have to think about the putt, the less time you
> have to doubt yourself."
>
> Vicki Goetze, LPGA Tour

Involuntary control. The last ingredient of a good routine is releasing voluntary control of the stroke and allowing your instincts to take charge. How often have you noticed that your putter was closed on the backswing and then tried to adjust, at the last second, by steering your blade through impact creating a push? This is an example of consciously controlling your putter and trying too hard to force it on line, which hurts your timing and natural rhythm. Practice to make your stroke reflexive. When you are playing let the instincts built on practice take over. Trying too hard to stroke the ball on line or make it, only causes you to tighten up and interfere with your natural stroke. PGA Tour player Larry Mize knows when he puts too much pressure on himself to make a putt. He said, "When I want to make a putt real bad, I know that's when I am in trouble. That's just not a good way to putt, you start putting pressure on yourself when you want to make it real bad . . . that is when you tighten up."

EXAMPLE PRESHOT ROUTINE FOR PUTTING

The following is an example of a preshot routine for putting, incorporating the six elements of a good putting routine. Of course, you should develop your own preshot routine. How you read a putt, the number of practice strokes you use, and the number of times you look at the hole will depend on your personality and personal preferences. We have separated the routine into physical and mental components. In reality, the corresponding elements blend together as one during a routine. Also, when you are playing, the components of a routine do not appear separate; they synthesize into one long behavior.

A Preshot Routine for Putting

Physical Aspect of Routine	Corresponding Psychological Skill
1. Standing behind the ball—assess the slope of green, distance from target, etc.	1. Take a deep breath to adjust arousal level and plan the shot.
2. Visually engage with the target from behind the ball.	2. Create mental blueprint of the ball rolling along intended line with the correct speed.
3. Approach the ball to set-up and take practice strokes.	3. Use self-talk and cue words to to build up confidence.

(continued)

A Preshot Routine for Putting (continued)

Physical Aspect of Routine	Corresponding Psychological Skill
4. Take a practice swing(s) next to the ball.	4. Physically and mentally rehearse the putt with the tempo that matches the putt.
5. Set-up and align putter and body to the target.	5. Visually engage with line of the putt.
6. Make final adjustments and glance at the target.	6. Release control to your body, trust your stroke.

MAINTAIN YOUR LINE

The biggest fault of amateur players is not selecting a specific line on which to hit the ball and not believing in their read. As discussed in Chapter 7, it's easy for you to change your decision about the break because of how your perception changes, and this leads to doubt and indecision. Select a line from behind the ball looking at the hole with your eyes about two feet or so above the green. This is the best place to sight your putt because your eyes are on the line of the putt and closer to the contours of the green. Don't change your mind when you get over the putt because the putt will look different when you read it from the address position.

> "You have to believe in your line if you want to have a good chance of sinking any putt."
>
> Greg Norman (1988), PGA Tour

REGROUP WHEN DISTRACTED

Many players lack the discipline to stop themselves from hitting a putt they are not ready to hit. Your routine should have a sense of flow and rhythm. If your routine is broken, so is your rhythm. Learn to recognize when you are not focused on the ball, cup, or line. Restart your routine from the beginning to regain your concentration. LPGA Tour pro Cindy Schreyer has learned to back off and start her routine over when distracted: "I have a routine that puts me in the proper focus and if I am not thinking about making the putt, then I need to back off. And I don't start at the point where I left off, I totally start over again because my routine was interrupted."

> "Once you get a routine down, you can feel something go wrong. Then you can make an adjustment real quick and it's easy to get back on track."
>
> Greg Kraft, PGA Tour

DEVELOP YOUR OWN PRESHOT ROUTINE

The specific behaviors and rhythm of your putting routine depend on at least three factors: your personality, personal preferences, and powers of imagination. Your personality will dictate the speed and rhythm of your routine. Usually, a relaxed, laid-back person will have a simple, slower moving routine like that of Fred Couples. A more time-conscious person will have a faster, more mechanical-looking routine like that of Chip Beck.

Your personal preferences dictate the amount and type of behaviors of the routine. For example, some players prefer to use only one practice stroke while others prefer to use three to gain a feel for the putt. How you aim and align yourself to the target will depend on what feels the most comfortable to you.

Lastly, your powers of imagination will influence the images you use to prepare yourself to putt. People differ in their use of images in their daily life. Some people learn with and relate better to visual images. Others learn better with feeling images, while others use a combination of both. If you are more visual, you should use visual images to create your mental blueprint for the putt. You should see the line of the putt and focus on the ball rolling along your intended line. If you relate better to feeling images, then you should use physi-

Develop a putting routine that is similar to your true personality and natural tempo.

cal feelings to create your mental blueprint. You should think more about tempo or contacting the ball solidly.

SHOULD YOUR ROUTINE BE ROUTINE?

When you first develop a routine for putting, it is anything but routine. You have to bring a high level of awareness to those rituals before they become ingrained into memory. With practice, your routine becomes routine and you complete it without conscious awareness. But once a routine becomes automatic does it lose its effectiveness? It depends on the player. Our experience tells us that some players think they perform better when their routine is automatic and they don't need to think about it. Other players like the security of a routine that requires conscious effort to perform.

Let us explain. If we change a player's preshot routine, it takes a great deal of concentration to ingrain the new routine. This can cause players to feel mentally "bound" to the routine, so much so that they forget the requirements of the shot. Some players complain that they become too focused or too obsessed with doing their routine just right, which takes them out of their normal rhythm. A routine can become a burden if a player worries too much about completing the routine correctly. This player is really distracting him or herself by worry-ing too much about the routine. With this type of player, a routine should become automatic and performed habitually, not be a source of distraction.

In other cases, changing a player's routine, and thereby making him or her think about performing a routine, is beneficial. Players, who are too mechanical, get ahead of themselves, or who often think negative thoughts can benefit from a preshot routine that is not habitual. Here, changing a player's routine helps him or her focus in the present moment, think positively, and stop overanalyzing.

MAKE YOUR ROUTINE SIMPLE TO FOLLOW

A routine should be a simple set of behaviors that you perform with minimal conscious awareness. Total concentration occurs when you are immersed in the requirements of the task to the point where time is suspended and you're in a state of flow. Wondering if you took the correct number of practice swings while you stroke your putt only hinders performance. Perfectionistic players can be too obsessed about doing the routine perfectly. A complicated routine can lead to confusion and overanalysis. The best thing you can do is simplify your routine and include only the basic elements that are necessary for good execution.

Try This!

Try this test to discover your imagery style and ability. Lie down in a comfortable position. Experience yourself playing golf at your favorite course. Try to recreate the experience as though you are reliving it. After you play two or three holes, ask yourself what type of images you created the most. Were you seeing your surroundings and the flight of the ball? Could you feel your body when you swung? How clear or lifelike were the images? The answer to these questions should give you a good idea of the images that you relate to the best. Integrate these images into your preshot routine for putting.

For example, if you rely more on visual images, practice seeing your ball roll along your line as you prepare to hit a putt. If you rely more on feel and touch, develop a sense of the distance and the tempo for the stroke and feel the ball to the hole before you hit a putt. If you like the sound of a solid putt, recreate the sound of solid contact and focus on that image. Work toward making your images realistic and lifelike.

The Child Within: Generating a Fearless Mindset

Most golfers either dread putting or enjoy putting. On most days, great putters are full of excitement when they approach a green. They are composed, confident, and love the challenge of making putts. The thought of failure rarely crosses their minds, and if it does, is quickly dismissed. Great putters love the opportunity to test their skills. They relish the feeling of immersing themselves in the act of putting and enjoying the moment. Great putters are fearless on the greens.

This is quite different for players who dread putting. For these people, putting is a torture from which there is no escape. Fearful putters develop excessive anxiety about their putting and never fully enjoy golf. They might enjoy the game of golf, but they despise putting. Frustrated by their putting, these players miss out on half the game. They play a game called "tee to green."

> "I love putting. You either win or lose on a putt, you get the result right then, it's clear cut."
>
> Greg Kraft, PGA Tour

In essence, putting is the ending to every hole in every round. You might be able to hit great shots from tee to green all day, but it doesn't matter if you can't capitalize on those shots. If every time you hit the ball well from tee to green and didn't score on the greens, you would be discouraged and frustrated with golf. If you dread putting, your challenge is to overcome fear and anxiety. By conquering your fear, you can enjoy the satisfaction of playing golf from tee to cup. The first step to winning your inner battle is to examine the origin of fear (or anxiety) and take corrective steps to resolve it.

"Fear is that little darkroom where negatives are developed."

Michael Pritchard

WHAT'S SO SCARY?

An element of being human is that you have feelings. Emotions like joy, sadness, happiness and fear are common to all people. Fear and anxiety have a useful purpose. In fact, fear is a coping mechanism for survival. Fear alerts us when an element of danger or threat is present, and prepares us to deal with it. However, fear can overwhelm us to the point of paralysis. In this state, productivity and performance are stifled. We describe anxiety as apprehension or worry about a potentially threatening situation. Fear is a form of extreme anxiety and is our reaction to a specific threat. The key to successful putting is to first identify what causes anxiety and fear, and second, deal with it head on.

Through evolution, humans developed a survival mechanism to cope with danger or threat to our well-being. Our reaction to a threatening situation is called the "fight or flight response." This response occurs when we feel threatened, either physically or psychologically. If danger is present, we go on alert. We deal with it by fighting or fleeing from the situation. To help us cope, the body releases chemicals into the bloodstream. Physiologically, a surge of adrenaline and other chemicals are instantaneously released and sent to the muscle groups to increase energy and sharpen attention. All of this happens so you can battle the stressor. People have documented this reaction with anecdotal stories of how parents perform superhuman acts of strength and courage when their children are in danger.

> **Fear, doubt, and anxiety all originate from negative pictures that you create in your mind.**

We know that in golf, you are not in physical danger, but you do become threatened psychologically. Your perception of the event is what triggers the fight or flight response. If you perceive an event as stressful or threatening, you become scared or anxious. If you perceive an event as joyful or benign, then you respond with a normal level of readiness or activation. A potentially threatening situation is only stressful when a person sees that situation as threatening. You create anxiety and fear, no one or no event makes you anxious or scared.

STRESS ON THE GREEN

When you feel pressure to make a putt, your fight or flight response kicks in. As you attempt to make a three-foot putt to win the match, you feel like your body wants to race, explode, or shut down. You feel your hands shake, your palms sweat, your breathing increases, your heart rate accelerates, and you can't think clearly. It's hard to putt well in this state. In this situation, you need to facilitate relaxation and change your perception of impending doom. Recognizing the origin of your anxiety and fear is a good place to start.

We learn about mistakes and eventually learn to fear mistakes from our teachers, coaches, and parents. For example, the educational system focuses on what students do wrong. When you make mistakes your teacher proclaims that you have failed to do something perfect. This corrective feedback is intended to help us learn, but it informs students that they have missed something or their answers are in error. Written on the top of your test was a minus one, minus two, and so on. Instead of pointing out how many you answered correctly, your teacher focused on the mistakes.

A similar scenario happens on the putting green. After a round of golf, most golfers remember the putts they missed, or lipped-out. Every time a putt doesn't go into the hole, a little reminder turns on in the golfer's head and yells "You missed! You made an error!" The central focus is not on how many good putts you made, but on the few that you missed. You practice all week trying to perfect your stroke and on game day or tournament day, your putting lets you down, or at least it appears so. These players think, "It could have been a good round, if only I hadn't missed those two short ones." If you focus on only the ones you missed, you are building a warehouse of negative pictures. If you do this long enough, you begin to expect to miss putts. Typically players don't remember the putts they made, instead they remember the putts they miss. As a result, they fear missing. If uncorrected, confidence is seriously affected.

Players forget that you can't make all your putts, and it's not always your fault that the putt didn't go in the hole. There are so many factors beyond your control that influence the outcome of any putt you hit. You can hit a great putt and still miss because an imperfection or spike mark threw the ball off line. The chances of making a five foot putt is less than 50 percent on perfect greens. As the distance increases, the odds of making it decrease.

What happens when players miss putts? Physically, they must either putt again or mark the ball. A truly confident player realizes that a miss is just a miss. A player who lacks confidence in this situation loses more confidence and becomes frustrated with putting. As this player stands over the next putt, memories of missing reinforce missing. Self-confidence dwindles. Beaten up by lip-outs and frustration, the player begins searching for a magical cure. This person changes his or her approach from day to day and his or her putting gets even worse.

A GOLFER'S BIGGEST ENEMY: THE FEAR OF MISSING

You build enduring putting confidence with a foundation of believing in yourself, trusting your ability, and making putts. Nothing deteriorates putting confidence faster than missing or by focusing on your misses. Missing putts is the primary factor driving players off the professional tours. This is also the number one reason golfers have a hard time beating their personal best scores.

Fear makes you focus on negative pictures and outcomes. But the good news is that you can choose a more effective way to view your putting. Memories of misses are in the past. Don't summon negative feelings associated with missing. Choose to live in the present and build new pictures of putting success, no matter what happened yesterday or on the hole before. Every putt is new. Thinking about the past only drains your mental energy. You can only control what happens in the present moment.

"A good putter may miss six eight-footers in a row, but he knows that he's going to make the next six putts."

Ernie Lanford, Florida State Golf Coach

Most players miss more putts during a round of golf than they make. Research conducted by Dr. Clyde Soley and others says that on a straight and level seven-foot putt, the top putters on tour only make 50 percent of their putts. Tour pros miss half of all seven-foot putts attempted on perfectly manicured greens.

We know that top putters miss even the shortest of putts. No one is immune to missing. Yet, we dread missing putts. A miss means that we have blown an opportunity to save a stroke or gain a stroke. A miss doesn't mean we made a mistake. Failure to make a putt doesn't make a person a failure. It merely records one particular unsuccessful attempt.

THE FEAR OF LOOKING STUPID AND INCOMPETENT

For one reason or another, golfers feel they look stupid or incompetent whenever the ball fails to go into the hole. This becomes especially true with shorter putts. A poor putter's self-talk brims with uncertainty and indecision. He or she realizes that it has a good chance of going in, but hears a voice of self-doubt saying "Don't miss this one; nobody misses these." The player focuses on the self-doubt and trying not to embarrass him or herself, instead of thinking about execution and the process of stroking the ball. In effect, players get in their own way.

DO YOU PROTECT YOUR EGO?

When players start to feel stupid about missing, they usually do several things to mask their misery. One way is to talk about how they weren't really trying to make it. Players who use this type of thinking always try to escape holing out or making short putts. They protect their score by not holing everything out. They always look for someone to "give" them their short putts. When tournament time rolls around, these players are the most likely to succumb to the pressure of short putts and not putt well. They become easily distraught early in the round after missing short putts that usually have been given to them. All along they have been fooling themselves into thinking they could make them in tournaments. In reality, they have cheated themselves out of the opportunity to build a foundation for real putting confidence.

Golfers use excuses to protect their ego when they miss. They blame the greens, the noise from playing partners, equipment—any excuse to save them from embarrassment. They may even laugh at their own ineptitude. With every miss, smile and snicker, there is a confident golfer dying inside. Laughing-off failure helps some golfers to somehow make it look better to others who may be watching. It is far better to seem unaffected than be embarrassed or humiliated by missing a short putt.

The notion of missing short putts when playing by yourself or with a friend is one thing, but when there is a small crowd of people watching, the pain of missing becomes intolerable. Perhaps the greatest fear humans have is embarrassing themselves in front of other people. This is why public speaking is difficult. People are afraid of looking stupid or saying something silly in front of a group of strangers. Their recognition, self-respect, and self-image are at stake.

The same is true on the golf course, but magnifies on the putting green. A player who can drive the ball straight down the middle of the fairway 250 yards and hit a four-iron within three feet of the cup, but who misses the putt, only becomes frustrated. The fear of missing and looking foolish becomes an intolerable situation. The situation becomes more obvious whenever substantial pressure or something is riding on the outcome. In these situations, players who fear putting are often at their worst.

THE FEAR OF CHOKING

Many golfers don't putt well under pressure. Pressure starts with the event, but ultimately it is your perception of an event that imposes pressure. If a player under pressure makes the putt, you can observe a general sense of relief on his or her face. If the player misses, and misses badly, the result is obvious. What you see is the total accumulation of pressure which has built up within the golfer.

> **Golfers who can't cope with pressure are choked by their own self-doubt and fear, and view putting as a death sentence.**

The worst thing that fellow golfers can do is to tell someone that they have just choked. Choking is the golfer's inability to perform consistently in competition due to fear, anxiety, or an inappropriate attentional focus. Most players have a specific choking point or choking threshold. This is the point at which a player stops acting naturally and automatically, and where fear takes over. What were once fairly easy shots, now become misses waiting to happen. Choking is more visible in the touch shots and putting.

Self-imposed pressure throws players over their threshold to a point of imbalance and their machinery breaks down. For many golfers, the weak link is their inability to make putts at crucial times in the match. Therefore, many golfers don't like to play competitive events. They would rather protect their ego than expose their weakness under public scrutiny. They would rather not risk choking.

You can see a player choke when he or she "stabs" or wishes a ball into the cup. What was once a smooth and confident stroke becomes a weak, glancing blow that never gives the ball a chance to get to the hole. Most putters who choke when they feel extreme pressure leave the ball well short of the hole. The self-labeling of being a choker on the greens does the most permanent damage. Once players are labeled chokers, they start to believe their title. They have a hard time getting rid of that label. The game is hard enough to master. You don't need these negative labels haunting you.

THE YIPS AND FREEZING

The biggest fear in golf is being afflicted with the "yips" or the "freeze." No matter where you go in the world of golf, you hear someone mention that they have the "yips." The "yips" is a devastating phenomenon in golf, and this may also lead to freezing.

Some golf theorists suggest that the yips are a compilation of missed putts which eventually take their toll on the player and lead to a total break-down of putting confidence. Others suggest that the yips are a part of a group of occupational disorders which include writer's cramps, violinist's syndrome, and computer programmer's disease. The hand and fingers become dis-jointed and uncontrollable when fine motor control and dexterity are needed. Thus, the sufferer is helpless. He or she can't function normally.

Short game guru, Dave Pelz, in his book, *Putt Like the Pros*, speaks of a neu-rosurgeon describing the "fail-safe mechanism within the human brain designed to protect the organism from tremendous stress." Milliseconds before human disaster, the brain shuts down as a protection mechanism so it is never conscious of what is happening. By shutting down immediately before putting, golfers don't realize what they have or haven't done. They are virtually blind to the cause or result.

Many theories for yipping have validity. From a neurophysiological per-spective, we don't know the exact triggering mechanism for twitching, flinch-ing, or ultimately yipping. We know for sure that the fear of missing exacerbates the fear of putting and they are linked to freezing and yipping.

We believe that yipping is the inability of the golfer to stabilize neuromuscu-lar control due to poor attentional focus or anxiety. Intense anxiety or fear does not allow the golfer to stabilize his muscular state and putt fluidly. Freezing occurs when the golfer is completely unable to draw the putter back and away from the ball and is unable to initiate the putting stroke. Most players with the yips can at least start the clubhead back and contact the ball. But freezing means the golfer is unable to start the club back; he or she is literally frozen over the ball. The player wants to move the club back, but his or her hands and arms are in a vise. It's like a deer that becomes frozen in the middle of the road by the fear of an approaching car. Freezing may be even more devastating than the yips, but both are curable. We don't believe that once you have them, you always have them. Several touring pro-fessionals and club pros who suffered from the yips have putted free again.

DEALING WITH FEAR ON THE GREEN

Are you an expert on missing putts? Have you missed so many putts in your career that you know just about every way to miss a putt? Thomas Edison tried about 10,000 times to perfect the light bulb. Edison was an expert on missing. When asked what was going wrong and how he finally found the right answer, he replied, "I failed so often, I finally ran out of ways to do it wrong." And "I was bound to succeed by virtue of all of my failures."

Thomas Edison persevered where others would have given up because of his belief in himself. Don't ever give up on yourself or your putting—no matter how bad it may be. Players who give up and say "I just can't putt any more," or "I just don't have it," have little chance of ever putting without fear. Better putting and overcoming fear comes from continually reminding yourself, "I am a good putter and I am continuing to get better."

> "A golf ball's a golf ball, a hole is a hole, a green is a green, it's all a matter of how you view the competition and how you handle it."
>
> Puggy Blackmon, University of South Carolina Golf Coach

Eliminate the Past

So you've missed several putts. You were an expert at missing putts, but your past doesn't have to control you now. You have to live in the present, not the past. Make the choice of becoming an expert at making putts. If you feel that you have tried just about every way to putt and still can't putt, it's time to evaluate your attitude. It probably isn't your equipment or technique that's lacking. The road to a putting overhaul starts on the path of total self-confidence and overcoming fear. You still "have it" within you.

Putt Like a Little Kid Again

We can learn so much from children. They play games without fear of social scrutiny or rejection. As a child, you were free to experience life with

Putting with a childlike attitude allows you to putt naturally and without fear.

no self-imposed constraints. You lived totally in the present moment without fear or anxiety. You were impervious to negative thinking. Fear and anxiety seemed like adult disorders. Little wonder why children putt so well. They putt free and totally in the present moment without the fear of consequences: the exact ingredients of great putting. They live for this moment. It doesn't matter what has happened previously or what will happen in the future. They don't let anything interfere with or distract them from what they are doing now.

It's a child's unrestricted attitude that allows them to putt without fear and accept whatever happens. It doesn't matter if the ball goes 10 feet past the hole. Judgement, criticism, and rejection from others aren't issues. They may become embarrassed, but it is just play. Have you ever seen children become frustrated and angry because they failed at play? Not likely. Children have a short-term memory when it comes to missing. You should, too.

Children are at play in the literal sense. If they miss, they move on with unhindered enthusiasm and positive expectation. They have the freedom to totally get into each new putt, and whether they miss it or make it, they go on with the same enthusiasm. Negative pictures, feelings, bruised egos, or embarrassments are not part of their world. They are too busy playing in the present to relive their past. If adults could play like kids, they would have a better chance of putting great. Adults, and especially those who play golf, need to learn to play as if there is no past or future. If we fall down and fail, we can always get back up and try again just like kids do. You can continue your current "adult" thinking, or you can think like kids do. Learn to be creative and free. Learn to putt like a kid again so you can putt naturally, without self-imposed restraints.

You probably know how to stroke the ball consistently. You also know how to read greens and identify undulations and breaks. You learned to hit an uphill putt with more effort and hit it softer on downhill putts. You know how to adjust for fast and slow greens. You will find no substitute for practice or experience. Take your experience and combine it with the carefree attitude of the child within you. No doubt, you will improve your putting.

> "I never feel like I have to make a putt, that puts too much pressure on yourself."
>
> Bob Estes, PGA Tour

THINK OF YOUR PUTT AS A "SECOND" ATTEMPT

How often have you hit a putt when you thought you were ready to putt, but missed it because you were nervous? Most of us hit the same putt again to see if we can make it on the second attempt. And the results are usually good. You probably have said, "Why didn't I do that on my first putt?" How were you able to make it the second time? Did you adjust your stroke to hit a better putt? Or did you relax and focus on a smooth stroke on the second try? Most likely you were more relaxed and fearless on the second attempt.

When you step up to a putt, it is a new putt with new meaning. Like many amateurs, when you play for a score, the outcome rests heavily on your mind. The thought of missing increases tension and this leads to controlling your stroke. The fear and tension caused by thinking about missing changes your normal, relaxed attitude and smooth stroke.

If the player drops a ball exactly where he or she putted the first putt, he or she usually makes it. The fear of missing, worry about score, or the thought of looking bad in front of friends and fellow competitors subsides. He or she then putts a second time from the same spot without any consequences. The stroke is smooth, flowing, relaxed and in control. This is why it makes sense to putt every putt like it's a second try. If you can get into a frame of mind like you do for that second try, your putting will improve. This mindset will help you focus on the process of being successful rather than fearing another miss. It helps you to forget about the outcome.

> "If you are obsessed with making a putt, it's a good chance you won't put a good stroke on it."
>
> Bob Burns, PGA Tour

REALITY CHECK ON THE GREEN

Years ago on tour, one of the best putters was Dr. Cary Middlecoff. During one of his poorer putting rounds, he reminded himself that if he didn't make the putt, his wife would still love him, his dog would still recognize him, and that his world wouldn't end. We feel this is healthy and rational advice for everyone who enjoys this maddening game. In fact, saying to your-self "There's more than 800 million people in the world who couldn't give a damn whether I make this putt or not," can put things into perspective. Giv-ing yourself a reality check lightens the burden of feeling like you have to make it.

> "You can't make it a situation where it's a 'have to' because you tighten up too much and it becomes unrealistic."
>
> Meg Mallon, LPGA Tour

BE YOUR OWN COACH

Many players hang on to the idea that confidence and trust will come after they make their first putt, but it just doesn't happen that way. Positive self-talk can be one of your most powerful assets on the course. Your self-talk should always be encouraging and supportive. Pump yourself up if necessary. Become your own coach on the putting green.

FOCUS ON THE TASK

If you feel pressure to make a putt, it simply means that you care. You care about the outcome because it's important to you. It also means you are human and you have feelings, thoughts, and emotions. If you didn't feel ner-vous in some situations, it probably means you don't care or are indifferent to those situations.

> "If you haven't made many putts all day, that's when you have to really focus on the process of executing and not worry about the outcome."
>
> Larry Mize, PGA Tour

Most of your fear relates to the outcome of an event—like missing a par putt to win a match. The fear causes players to get ahead of themselves rather than focus on the task. The best way to deal with the pressure to make a putt is to separate the task from the consequences of your actions. Focus on what you can control, which is execution and staying in the present. Once your club contacts the ball, it's out of your control. Your task is to stroke the ball on line, not avoid a miss.

Try This!

The following tips will help you overcome anxiety and fear during putting. Try one or all of these strategies for 14 consecutive days. You will improve your ability to handle pressure putting by focusing on the task and hitting a solid putt.

Tip No. 1. Focus on the Process

Whenever you approach an important putt, delete the outcome from your mind. Forget about the past and the consequences of making it or missing it. Focus on what you have to do to hit a solid putt on your line. Think only about good execution. Focus on your routine and rolling the ball on your line or with good speed.

Tip No. 2. Maintain a Continuous Putting Routine

Players doubt themselves and lose confidence when they stall or freeze over the ball. This allows tension to creep into their arms, hands, and shoulders. Don't spend too much time over the ball because this increases self-doubt, anxiety, and indecision. Maintain a rhythmic and continuous motion throughout the entire preputt and putting phase. Maintain motion with your body, hands, or eyes to keep your routine fluid. If you do not have a putting routine, see Chapter 8 for developing yours today.

Tip No. 3. Take Deep Abdominal Breaths

One way to stabilize yourself when stressed is to consciously relax yourself. Breathing is an excellent way to return your hyper body and mind to a normal state. Take two or three deep breaths while reading your putt from behind the ball. Take another deep breath while moving to address the ball. Breathe through your lower abdominal cavity. Finally, when you are taking your last look at the hole, relax your arms and grip pressure and exhale completely. This allows you to make a very smooth and unhurried stroke.

Tip No. 4. Putt Without Delay

When you take your last look from target to ball, refocus as quickly on the ball as possible and putt without delay. This helps you keep a strong visual image of your target and promotes a reflexive action, which prevents you from freezing. Start the putter head back immediately after you refocus on the ball. This acts as a form of visual trigger or visual forward press. You also can use a forward press to initiate the stroke. After refocusing on the ball, push your hands slightly forward to the target and then start the putter head back. This prevents you from focusing on the putter head during the backswing and becoming "ball-bound." Finally, try putting while looking at the hole. Trust your stroke. Beginners who started putting this way putt just as well as they would using the conventional method.

Tip No. 5. Focus on a Specific Part of the Ball

Players who hit putts squarely, and focus on a specific part of the ball, roll the ball better. If you are nervous about making a putt, try using this technique. You have to hit the ball squarely to insure the ball rolls the proper distance. The ball tends to hold its line better also. You can focus on the back half of the ball, a number or letter, or on a dimple on the ball. Use a visual anchor and hit the ball solidly.

Tip No. 6. Putt with Total Trust and Assertiveness!

Stroke the ball with trust and assertiveness. Do not putt the ball until you are confident and comfortable. Forget about mechanics or how to stroke the ball. Back away and start over if you are unsure of yourself. Be aggressive with the putt and live with the results. Great putting is about focusing on what you have to do to make putts, not about trying to avoid missing and three putting.

Preparing Your Mind to Putt Your Best

G reat putting involves several important factors, including the ability to read greens, visualize the line of a putt, and believe you can make it. When you get on a roll, psychological momentum and confidence give you a boost and help you play even better. The opposite is also true. When you don't play well and things are not going your way, poor play can cause you to talk yourself into playing worse.

Why can't players always play with confidence and positive momentum? The positive cycle must break down somewhere or players would always have confidence and putt better and better. For most amateurs and some professionals, one or two bad putts or shots can interrupt momentum. A loss of momentum causes a player's mind to become filled with doubt and this leaves more room for indecision and hesitation, and indecision generates a poor putting stroke. Soon, the player is on a "downward spiral." If the player misses one or two more putts, he or she thinks the putting has gone sour and expects bad putting to continue.

How often after you finish playing do you recall the putts you missed and the ones you should have made that you didn't? You say "I should have shot better today." Do you remember the 30-footer you holed on number 15? Do you remember the putts you holed to save par? Usually not. Most players think about the putts they missed and analyze how the round "could or would" have been better if they didn't miss those two easy putts. This type of thinking has a negative effect on your confidence.

INSTILLING CONFIDENCE: A NEVER-ENDING PROJECT

Some players unknowingly sabotage themselves mentally. The night before a match these players think about how to avoid looking stupid and not embarrassing themselves the next day. They fear what others think if they play poorly. Players who sabotage themselves also look for excuses to play badly before they tee the ball. They say, "It's too windy," or "The greens are too bumpy," or "I feel tired today." Creating excuses gives players built-in reasons to play poorly and often causes them to look for bad breaks and other incidents that support why they can't make putts.

Preparing your mind to play well in competition includes maintaining confidence in your putting off the course. Off the course, what percentage of your thoughts are about putting great? And what percentage of your thoughts are about putting poorly or trying to find a way to not embarrass yourself on the course? Do you think about the three short putts you missed yesterday, or do you think about the ones you made? Do you carry an image of yourself as a poor putter?

The last thing you should do is arrive at the course and look for reasons to fail and putt poorly. If you missed your first putt, how would you respond given your present attitude? Do you say, "It isn't my day," and give up early in the round? A better alternative is to think about the good reasons you have to putt your best. How many successful putts have you hit in practice? You must have had great putting rounds in the past. Think about how many putts you made in pressure situations. You have to focus on "I have done it in the past and can do it again." With this attitude, even if you miss your first two putts, you can still give yourself a chance to make your next putt. Focus on the strengths of your putting and build your game around what you do well.

THE POSITIVE COACH INSIDE YOU

Each of us can be our own ally or enemy. You can give yourself a pep-talk and tell yourself that you can putt well on any given day or you can criticize and tell yourself that you can't. You can dismiss what others tell you about your putting by ignoring them, but you can't ignore what you say to yourself.

Your self-talk can be an asset or a liability. Always talking to yourself negatively by saying, "You're not a good putter," "You can't putt well," and "You never will be a good putter," wears on you. Give yourself a break and talk to yourself like a champion, not like a loser. Tell yourself that you can putt well, you have putted well, and you will putt well until you begin to truly believe it. One of the best putters on the Tour, Greg Kraft, constantly uses self-talk to help him stay focused on the greens. He reminds himself to select a line, stay committed to that line, and trust what his eyes see. He even uses self-talk to give himself a kick in the pants when he is not concentrating well. He "tightens" his focus and raises his intensity by giving himself a pep-talk.

PICTURES ARE WORTH A THOUSAND PUTTS

The best way to mentally prepare yourself for putting well is to picture yourself making putts. It's a boost to your confidence when you create images of yourself making putt after putt. Recall when you had your best putting round. What were you experiencing? Did you feel in control? Did you concentrate well? Did you believe you could make every putt? What started the belief that you could make everything?

Use the thoughts and emotions when you were putting your best to your advantage. Feed off those pictures by seeing yourself playing your next round with the same positive emotions and thoughts. Relive your best putting round and imagine putting with the same focus and confidence in your next round. Experience yourself on the first green, reading the putt, picking a line, going through your routine, and holing the putt. Build a memory bank of great putting by seeing yourself hole putt after putt.

> **Imagining yourself putting well builds self-confidence and reinforces trust in your putting ability.**

DON'T EXPECT TO PUTT PERFECTLY

How often have you started a round with the expectation to play and putt well and then not played to your expectation? Having high expectations usually has a negative effect on your game. If you expect to play well, it instills confidence. But if your play isn't up to par with your expectations, it's easy to become frustrated and see your effort as a failure. You never want to expect to play poorly; that hurts confidence. But if your expectations are too high, you set yourself up for failure. The first bad shot or putt you hit can ruin your round because you're not playing like you expected to play.

> "Accept the fact that you're probably never going to putt as well as you think you ought to."
>
> Jack Nicklaus, Senior PGA Tour

Most players play their best when they don't have expectations about how well they will play. You can hit 18 perfect putts, but the probabilities of making them all are small because there are random or chance factors that influence the outcome of any putt. You can make every putt, but expecting to make all of your putts is unrealistic. Having a belief that you can make each putt is a better option. The proper attitude says, "I can make every putt, but I don't assume I will make every putt." Believe that you are going to make it, but accept the fact that you can hit a great putt and it may not go in the hole.

PREPARING TO PUTT WELL IN TOURNAMENTS

Tournament play usually makes amateur players get more serious, controlled, tense and anxious. The pressure they put on themselves makes golf a different game. In a player's mind, the task changes, but it's really the same task. It's the same golf course, with the same number of holes, and the same assignment. Your perception of the event is the only thing that changes your outlook. A simple three-foot putt becomes a life-or-death situation.

You have to prepare your mind to approach each putt the same way you hit putts on the practice green. The task has not changed. You have to read the putt, pick a line, believe you can make it, and let the stroke happen. What usually happens is that players get too absorbed in results and how they are doing in the tournament. Prepare for your next tournament by making it a goal to treat each putt the same and don't get caught up in what the putt means if you miss or make it. Make a commitment to address each putt as a challenge to focus on the task. The end result is not directly under your control.

COPING WITH POOR PUTTING

Even the best putters in the world have poor putting days. The key is that they know how to react when the putts don't fall. This allows professional players to turn a 75 into a 71 and amateurs to turn an 85 into a 79. You need a system for dealing with those days when you don't have good touch. To do this, think back to how you typically react when the putts don't fall. List your typical responses. This may include: I get frustrated and try even harder to make putts, or I lose concentration, or I lose confidence and feel that I can't make anything.

Once you understand how you respond when not putting well, you can choose the best way to handle the situation to help you finish the round without making it worse. Here are a few suggestions you can practice to prepare yourself when the putts don't fall:

Don't let frustration affect your ball striking. Poor putting can cause you to pressure other parts of your game and try harder. A bad putting day can cause you to be more aggressive in other parts of your game. You pressure yourself to hit it closer or chip it closer to the pin. To do this, you have to drive the ball longer, so you have a shorter shot to the green. Soon, your poor putting works its way back to your entire game.

Treat each putt as a new opportunity to make one. Forget the past, it's over with. You have to let go of past lip-outs, three-putts, and missed three-footers, and treat each putt like it is your first and last putt. Hit each putt as if it were a new chance to make a good stroke.

Think that the next putt you make will spark your putting. Experience yourself on the golf course having a bad putting day. Then, imagine yourself feeling like the next putt is the one that sparks your round and gets you putting well. See yourself go through your routine with confidence and optimism. Look for a way to gain momentum instead of reasons why you should expect to miss the rest of the day.

Just do your task, forget about result. It can be very frustrating when you miss. This is when you have to remind yourself that missing is part of the game. You are going to have days when you hit several good putts that don't fall in the cup; that's just part of golf. You can do everything right and still miss. It's just a fact that you are going to misjudge a few reads. If you can launch the ball on your line with the correct speed, then you are successful! It's out of your hands at that point.

Play the odds game. Another method for coping is playing the odds game. This is an attitude that says the more you miss, the better the odds that you will make your next putt. If a basketball player is a 70 percent free-throw shooter, and he misses his first four free throws, the chances are that he will make his next three.

Stick with your routine. Imagine yourself playing your next round. The putts are not falling. The tendency is to search for a remedy to the problem, when there may not even be a problem. You may take more time or less time, focus on stroke path, or change your routine. Instead, experience yourself doing your preshot routine when the putts are falling. See yourself playing with your normal pace and flow. Don't let missing change your approach to making putts. If you need to adjust, change your ball position or posture. Check your basics, but don't alter how you prepare for each putt.

Tell yourself to have patience. Maybe the most important quality in putting is patience. Experience yourself becoming frustrated with a bad putting day. Then, imagine yourself when you are patient during a good day. Know that the

---

Patience is a form of putting confidence that allows you to remain unaffected by frustration and missed attempts.

putts will start to drop soon. You can list several reasons a putt doesn't find the cup and beat yourself up for missing, but it doesn't have to be that way if you take control.

WHAT ARE YOUR GOALS?

An excellent method of preparing your mind for the next round is to focus on what you want to achieve. Goals focus your mind in a positive way on what you want to accomplish. Instead of thinking about how not to mess up your next round, goals help you focus on the process of performing well.

Goals are what drives your behavior on the course. What are your goals for the next round? Your goal may be to putt well, but don't you first need to decide what you have to do to putt well? You can have several different goals for putting. You might want to set an outcome goal like number of putts per round. A better option is to focus on performance or process goals. Examples of process goals include rolling the ball well on each putt, hitting your putt on your intended line, sticking to your preshot routine, or maintaining patience on each putt. Setting process goals helps you focus on the task of hitting good putts and gets you away from focusing on results or consequences of results.

Try This!

Select one goal you need to focus on to help you putt your best. Think of something you haven't been doing well lately, such as trusting your read and putting stroke. Imagine yourself playing your next round with the level of trust that you want to play with. Experience yourself going through your preshot routine and stroking the ball with trust on every putt. As you prepare for your next round, make it your goal to trust what you see.

Productive Putting Practice: Taking It to the Course

Are great putters born or made? Some players are gifted with great touch and soft hands, while others work at being great putters. To be a truly great putter, we think that you must possess a fair amount of hand-eye coordination and fine-muscle control, but to be the best that you can, you also must develop those physical abilities through practice. You cannot change your genetics, but you can improve how much you practice and the quality of that practice. Practice is essential for grooving your stroke, developing touch and feel, gaining confidence in your method, and understanding how putts react.

Physical practice is an excellent way to improve your confidence in putting if it is quality practice. How you practice influences how much you learn and transfer to the course. Putting practice is more than just mindlessly hitting putts to different holes on the practice green. Our experience and research in sport psychology tell us that your practice will be more efficient when it is similar to the actual competitive situation. This requires you to use your imagination and concentrate when you practice putting.

"If I didn't practice a lot, I wouldn't be as good a putter as I am. For me the bottom line for confidence comes from practicing."

Larry Mize, PGA Tour

THE DIFFERENCE BETWEEN PRACTICING AND PLAYING

The goal of putting practice is to train yourself to putt well in competition, but we don't think average players approach it this way. Many good players putt well on the practice green, but can't putt well on the course. These players don't hit practice putts to putt well on the golf course.

One practice goal should be to groove a putting stroke that is consistent and repeatable. More important, your goals should be to develop feel and touch, learn to trust your stroke, and gain confidence in your method and ability to make putts on the course. The primary goal should be to build competence and confidence, yet most players practice to practice stroke mechanics.

On the course, the goal is to get the ball into the hole any way you can. This requires throwing away mechanics and putting with confidence, focus, and trust. To do this you need to practice your stroke to the point that it is a habit so you can put yourself on autopilot on the course.

"It's very hard to putt well during a round if you have mechanical thoughts."

Larry Mize, PGA Tour

The best putters in the world think that putting is more mental than physical, and we agree. Once you step on the course, you must forget stroke mechanics and stop watching your putter head. Too many players focus on mechanics and never learn to trust their method, which causes them to steer their stroke. It's too late to practice your stroke on the course. You have to play with what you practiced and let your natural stroke come out. The more mechanical you are, the more awkward your stroke feels. Great putters trust their putting. They have a few fundamentals to which they keep, but most of it is sheer confidence and knowing they will make it.

TRANSFERRING YOUR PUTTING TO THE COURSE

The most efficient way to practice your putting is to practice under the conditions you encounter on the course. If you practice in situations that simulate play on the course, you will putt better on the course.

"You are going to get more out of your practice, making it more like what it is going to be on the course."

Bob Estes, PGA Tour

Practice on similar greens. One challenge all golfers face that other athletes don't is adjusting to different playing surfaces and conditions. Adjusting to different green speeds is the biggest challenge for tour pros. This requires that you practice on greens similar to the tournament greens, and develop a specific touch for those greens. This is called specificity training. If you practice on slow greens and play on a course with fast greens, you will hit several putts long because you ingrained a different touch. If the greens on the course have many knolls, practice on similar greens. That way you develop the correct feel and touch for the greens and understand how the ball will react on those greens.

Practice several different lengths. Putt several different length putts of 10, 20, 30, and 40 feet, and all distances in between. If you practiced only 10-footers every day how well would you putt from 30 feet? Not very good. Vary your distances often. If you are going to hit 50 putts, don't hit them all from 10 feet. Hit as many different length putts as you can so when you get on the course, you won't have to hit a putt that feels unfamiliar.

Practice different breaks. Vary the type and severity of breaking putts. Hit left-to-right breaking putts. Hit right-to-left breaking putts. Hit putts that have large breaks. Hit putts that have small breaks. Hit putts with double breaks. Change the length of each of the breaking putts also. Hit putts uphill and downhill.

When you practice different breaking putts, it helps you to visualize those putts better, and this helps improve touch. Breaking putts require both touch and imagination. The clearer you can see or sense how a putt breaks, the more

> **Mentally practicing pressure situations helps you cope with pressure on the course.**

confident you will feel when it's time to stroke the putt. Don't just practice your strengths in putting. If you have difficulty with left-to-right putts, spend more time practicing them.

> "If I practice the right way, then normally I feel prepared and then I have confidence."
>
> Vicki Goetze, LPGA Tour

Simulate pressure situations. The best way to learn how to take your practice putting to the course is to simulate pressure situations you encounter on the course. One way to do this is by playing mind games with yourself. Imagine you have to make a five-foot putt for par on the last hole to win the club championship, or better yet to win the U.S. Open. Think about trying to make a ten-foot putt for birdie to win the Masters.

Another way to simulate pressure is to invent drills in which the pressure builds as you progress. Greg Norman uses a drill where he has to hit 25 putts in a row starting at two feet and then progressing to three, four, five, and six feet. The pressure mounts as you get closer to the last few putts because if you miss, you must start over. Try playing 18 holes on the practice green with a friend and making a friendly wager.

Practice to make everything. Most great putters practice to make all their putts on the practice green. They address a putt on the practice green just like a putt on the course. Great putters use the same preshot routine and practice with the same intensity as they use on the golf course. Many players prefer to use only one ball when they practice because that's what happens on the course.

> "When you practice with one ball, one chance, one hole, then it is more the way it is on the course."
>
> Bob Estes, PGA Tour

MAKE IT AUTOMATIC

Mechanical players sometimes have trouble feeling comfortable with their stroke so when they play, they can't trust their stroke. These players practice stroke too much, they don't practice to make putts. They focus on the path of the stroke when they play and this makes it hard to think about holing putts. They put too much emphasis on the technique of perfect mechanics thinking that is the key to making putts. They can't let go of their control and do what comes naturally. You develop faith in your stroke by practicing it and knowing that it is solid enough to make putts. You have to forget mechanics as you get closer to playing a match, and especially when you go play. The more you practice trust, the easier it is to putt instinctively on the course.

What does it mean to practice trust? Trust is giving up conscious control of the stroke and allowing your body to do what you have practiced. Trusting your stroke means focusing on your line or the hole and letting yourself hit the target without thinking about how to hit it there. It means letting go of your cognitive, analytical mind and letting feel and instinct take over. A player who trusts his or her stroke does not think about body position, swing path, or putter head position. This player is thinking about ball, line, roll, and speed.

> "I don't worry about position, I just walk in behind a putt, wiggle around until I get comfortable and then I hit it."
>
> Bob Murphy, Senior PGA Tour

PRACTICE FOR TOUCH AND FEEL

The great putters that we work with all believe that having good touch and feel is necessary for great putting. You can't have confidence on the greens without a good sense of touch. Why is touch so important? Touch controls speed, and having the right speed is half the equation in great putting. You must have the touch to leave the ball close to the hole on longer putts. But touch also dictates the line you select on breaking putts. On breaking putts, you have to hit a putt with the right speed in order for it to take the correct amount of break you planned. If hit too hard, a putt won't take the break, if hit too soft, a putt won't hold its line.

Most players would say that touch and feel are the same—the ability to control speed or distance. Personally, we define feel as continuous sensory feedback you receive through your sensory receptors. For example, when you stroke a putt, you receive instantaneous feedback about the length of your stroke or how the putter felt at impact. Visually, you see how far the ball traveled. This type of feedback helps you learn and develop touch.

> "Speed is the most critical element in putting, and touch is what regulates that speed."
>
> David Edwards, PGA Tour

We store several kinds of images in our memories including visual, kinesthetic (feeling), auditory, and olfactory images. Touch is the ability to use images (developed from your composite experience) to hit a putt with the correct distance. For example, standing over a 30-foot putt, you recall an image of what a 30-foot putt feels like, and then try to reproduce that image. You need both feel and touch for good putting. You must receive feedback through sensory input (feel) to develop kinesthetic images (touch) that allow you to control your speed.

Some players inherently develop better touch and feel because they have keener motor abilities, like hand-eye coordination and fine-muscle control. But any player can improve touch and feel through practice. Without ever hitting a putt, you have no experience of what it feels like to hit a putt 20 feet on a flat green. That's why you see beginners hitting a 20-foot putt 10 feet past the hole. As you practice and log putts in your memory, you begin to associate a 20-foot putt with a certain feeling. The more experiences you have logged in memory, the better touch you have and the better recall you have of the feeling of a 20-foot putt.

The goal of practice is to develop your sense of feel and touch. The best way to achieve this is to hit putts from several different distances, or better yet, every possible distance. If you only practiced 20 footers, how would you gauge a 40-foot putt? If you only practiced uphill putts, how well would you hit downhill putts? Hitting putts from longer distances will promote your touch on the greens. The more you vary the lengths, the faster you enhance your feeling on the greens. Judging the speed of a putt by measuring the length of your backstroke (taking it back two inches, four inches, etc.) is a mistake.

"The most important thing about great putting is speed. Launch is the second most important thing, having the ball start where you want it to go."

Bill Glasson, PGA Tour

A better option is to think about the tempo of the stroke or the feeling of the stroke. As you practice from various distances, tune into the feeling of your arms, the acceleration of your hands, and the feeling of the putter impacting the ball. Close your eyes as you stroke the ball. This helps heighten your physical sensations as you stroke the ball and accelerate learning.

Eyes closed drill. One drill for developing feel is to putt to different targets with your eyes closed. When you close your eyes, it forces you to tune into physical sensations. Place four tees at distances of 10, 20, 30, and 40 feet. As you hit each putt with your eyes closed, quickly estimate if the putt is short, long or a just right (12–18 inches past the hole). After the ball leaves your blade, estimate its distance. Try hitting ten balls to each of the four targets.

Staggered tee drill. Another drill is to hit each putt a different distance than the last. Place five tees at different distances; start with 20, 25, 30, 35, and 40 feet. Your goal is to hit the ball past the first tee, but no more than two feet past. Putt to all targets, changing the distance each time. If you miss one, you have to start over. When you get to the final tee, work back to the first tee. Practice this drill using different distance targets.

Maximum touch drill. Hit one putt after the other, with each putt being a little longer than the next. Start with five feet. Hit a putt five feet, then hit your next putt just past the last putt, hitting putts slightly longer and longer. Roll the next putt past the last putt, but as close to it as possible, and so on. See how many balls you can roll inside 50 feet. You can reverse the drill. Start at 50

Tune up your touch and feel for the greens by putting to various targets during warm-up.

feet and hit the next putt inside the first putt, hitting each putt shorter and shorter. Test yourself to see how many balls you can pack into 50 feet. The closer you hit the balls together on each successive putt, the better your touch.

IMPROVING CONFIDENCE WITH SHORT PUTTS

Hitting several long putts from various distances is great for developing touch and building confidence, but confidence also comes from practicing short putts. Many great putters say that they like to hit short putts (in the four to six foot range). These are the putts you hit most often on the course. The fact that you make most putts from this length helps build confidence.

Seeing and hearing the ball go in the hole time after time improves confidence for anyone. Vicki Goetze told us she gains confidence by hitting 100 short putts in a row. It's part of her daily routine, which instills confidence on the golf course. This helps when she stands over a three-foot putt on the course; she knows it's going in the hole.

TAKING IT TO THE COURSE

The best type of practice is the kind that helps you consistently perform on the golf course. Every putt you hit on the golf course is essentially a new putt with a new distance, speed, break, and visual appearance. But most of us don't practice in a way that is specific to what happens during a round of golf. The more experience you have with hitting different putts, the better prepared you will be when you get on the course.

> "Perfect practice makes perfect; if you practice the wrong thing, you just get good at the wrong thing."
>
> David Edwards, PGA Tour

Do a little each day. The first principle for maximizing learning is to spread your practice sessions over several days instead of devoting an entire day to putting only. It's better to practice your putting a little each day than to cram your practice into one long session. A practice session that is too long can lead to fatigue, and fatigue impairs learning. Practicing a little each day leads to better learning and transfer, because your motor system remembers better with this type of schedule.

Vary the type of putt. Vary the type of putts you hit during a session, and the order in which you practice them. Don't just hit 10-foot, uphill putts. Practice hitting putts from several different distances and various breaks. With a breaking putt, practice lagging the ball into the side of the hole and hitting the same putt firm into the front of the hole. See how many different ways you can make the same putt; experiment with the line and the speed of each putt. Change your practice routine from day to day. Start with long putts one day and then short putts the next day.

Practice like you play on the course. Most players just hit putt after putt from the same place on the practice green. After two or three putts you know how the putt breaks. Then, the task is to putt the ball on line. That's great for practicing your stroke, but that is not effective practice. Each putt is new on the course. It requires a new read, set-up, and touch. Prepare for each putt the same as you prepare for a putt on the course. Read each putt, go through your preshot routine, set-up and align to the hole, and stroke the ball like it is your last putt on the green. This is the way you normally play, why not practice the same way?

Practice with a purpose. Set goals and practice with a purpose. Goals increase persistence and push you to perform your best. Select a specific goal for each drill you do in practice. For example, place 10 balls in a circle, three feet around the hole. Your goal is to make all 10 putts in a row. When you accomplish this goal, make it more difficult by moving farther away or using more balls. Revise your goals often and make them more challenging as you improve your putting.

Practice all parts. Practice your weaknesses as well as your strengths. Golfers, like other athletes, like to practice their strengths. It gives them a sense of accomplishment and fulfillment. That's OK. But, if you want to be the best putter possible, you have to discipline yourself to work on your weaknesses. If you have trouble lagging the ball from long-range, you should spend more time on this part of your putting. Start your practice session on this part of your game when your concentration is sharp and you are still fresh.

THE USE OF VISUAL AIDS DURING PRACTICE

Putting is a very visual task. The better you can see a line to the hole, and aim and align yourself to a target, the more putts you will likely make. Many good putters use visual aids to help develop better images of the line of a putt and to practice aiming and aligning themselves better. Some players putt on a chalk line to help them see the line better. For breaking putts, you can place a string on the ground that matches your putting line. Other players practice short putts between two parallel clubs placed on the ground to give them a sense of a channel all the way to the hole. The advantage of using visual aids is you get more specific and faster feedback about how well you hit a putt, and this leads to faster learning and better performance.

Try This!

The next time you practice your putting, use just one ball. Putt to 18 different targets or holes and finish every hole. Stroke each putt like you have only one chance and it's your last putt. Read each putt like you would on the course and use you entire preshot routine. Practice to make each putt.

The Golden Touch: Warming Up Your Putter

Most amateur players we know neglect a putting warm up before playing. They arrive at the course 10 minutes before tee time, put on their shoes, and walk directly to the first tee without warming up. And then they wonder why they three-putted the first two greens. Professionals would never consider playing a competitive round without a routine warm-up. They know exactly how much time they need for warm-up and have a specific routine before they tee off.

A warm-up has three important purposes: focusing your mind, instilling confidence, and gaining a feel for the speed of the greens. A warm-up is similar to stretching for a sprinter. It helps you gain the correct attentional mindset and prepare your mind for physical activity. The warm-up also primes the muscles used for putting. It allows you to gain a sense of rhythm and comfort with your stroke.

The warm-up should also be used to build confidence and reassure yourself that you can make putts. You have to feel comfortable on the course to make putts. And comfort transfers into confidence. You gain a sense of comfort on the practice green. Your real test comes when you hit the first putt. To give yourself the best chance at making that putt, you want to feel like you are ready to make it.

Most importantly, a warm-up helps you test the speed and break of the green and develop a sense of touch. The speed and texture of putting greens change from course to course because of varying types of grass, grains, undulations, and length of grass. Even the speed of the greens on your home course can change each day, depending on how the greens were cut that day or the weather conditions. If you are playing a different course from the previous round, your biggest challenge is to adjust to the speed of the greens. The preround warm-up may be the only time you have to adjust your touch.

GENERATE YOUR FEEL ON THE GREEN

The best way to develop your feel and gain a sense of touch is to hit several long putts to various targets. You want to start with 30-, 40-, and 50-foot putts. See how close you can lag the ball to the hole. You may not have any putts of that distance, but that is the best way to sense the speed and adjust your touch on the green. Hit long putts from both above and below the hole.

Next, hit several long, breaking putts to give you a sense of how much your ball breaks on the green. Hit right-to-left putts, hit left-to-right putts, with big and small breaks. Carefully watch how the ball breaks on the green. You are not necessarily trying to make putts here. Instead, you are tuning your feel for the greens.

VALIDATE YOUR CONFIDENCE

As stated earlier, a primary goal of a warm up is to feel confident in your ability to make putts. This means you should putt the ball on line and hit your target. Your confidence can erode when you are trying to make putts and don't make any. You want to see positive images and create a mental backlog of putts that dive into the hole. When you step over your first putt of the day, it helps to have

Validate Your Confidence

Create positive images of success by holing a series of short putts during your putting warm-up.

a fresh image of the ball diving into the hole. Don't be afraid to make putts on the practice green. If you say to yourself "save those putts for later," know that you will have many more good ones for the course.

The best method for developing positive images is to hit several putts of three feet or less. As you hit putts into the hole, you see the ball go in, you hear the ball go in, and you feel the ball go in. This builds fresh images in your mind, which make you feel comfortable when it is time to play.

The last thing you should do is doubt your stroke and start focusing on the mechanics of your stroke. It's too late to change your stroke. You have to go with what you practiced. Focus more on reading the green, seeing the correct line, and letting your stroke happen.

MORE IS NOT ALWAYS BETTER

The amount of time spent warming up on the practice green should be specific to each person's needs. Some players feel more comfortable hitting a few putts to get a feel for the green and going to the first tee. Others prefer to spend more time warming up to gain a sense of tempo and touch.

Ten to 15 minutes should be sufficient to hit several long and short putts. If you are an experienced player, you probably have a set routine and know how much time you need to warm up before playing. If you don't have a system for preparing yourself to putt, we recommend that you start today. This way you know how much time you need. When you finish your warm-up, you're done.

More is not always better when it comes to the time you spend preparing. You want to tune your focus to the task of putting, but you don't want to tax your concentration powers. A warm-up that is too long can drain your energy and hurt your focus on the course. Save it for the course. Spend a few minutes of quality, focused time to feel comfortable, and then go. You shouldn't have to make five ten-footers in a row before you can walk to the first tee.

GO WITH WHAT YOU HAVE

Your preround warm-up is only a tune-up for what is to follow; it's not practice. This is the wrong time to practice your stroke. It's too late to change or work on mechanics now. That's like cramming for a test just before the test starts. You don't want to doubt your stoke now. A little doubt can make some players adjust their ball position, posture, or alignment, or even fiddle with their stroke. You can't change the motor program for your stroke in ten minutes, so go with what you have practiced.

If you haven't putted well recently, the tendency is to practice your stroke, which causes you to think about mechanics on the course. You might try making only a small adjustment in your stance or ball position. Better yet, find a swing key that will help you gain stroke tempo. The best option would be to hit several short putts to instill confidence before you play.

ONE-, TWO-, OR THREE-BALL WARM-UP?

People differ in their philosophies about how many balls they use during warm-up. Should you putt with only one ball since that is what you do on the course? Or should you putt with three balls so you can hit more putts in a given time? Some players have a strong argument for warming up with only one ball. Practicing with one ball is more specific to what you do on the course. You only have one shot on the course so why not tune your focus to how you play on the course? Second, it forces you to hit a different putt each time. When you have three balls, you can repeat the putt three times in a row, and give yourself more chances to make it.

> "You don't get two chances on the course, you just get one, so putt with one ball."
>
> Bob Estes, PGA Tour

Most players use two or three balls when they warm up. You can see advantages with this method. Using three balls allows you to hit more putts in a given time, especially long putts. Using three balls also allows you to adjust your touch on longer putts. If you leave the first putt short, you can putt to the same cup and adjust your tempo or feel for the putt. Also, the first putt gives you an indication of the correct line of the putt, and the second or third balls test your ability to launch the ball on that line.

REMEMBER, IT'S ONLY A WARM-UP

A priority of warm-up is to build confidence and fine-tune your concentration. If you don't putt well in warm-up, don't let it bother you and don't talk yourself into putting poorly on the course. Many players don't putt well in practice because their concentration has not peaked. For some, it's easier to focus when they get into competition and are excited to play. Don't let a poor warm-up hurt your confidence to make putts that day. Remember a warm-up is just a warm-up, it's not a competition.

Don't count how many putts you make or miss during your warm-up. It's a time to develop feel and test the speed of the greens. If you hate missing putts in warm-up, don't hit the ball to a target. Work on your speed and distance control. Then hit two- or three-footers to gain confidence that you can make putts.

Try This!

Develop a consistent warm up routine on the putting green before you play a round. For the next two weeks, stick to that warm up routine. Create a routine that feels comfortable for you. If you have a chance to go to a professional tournament, observe how the pros warm up before a round. We suggest you start with a few long putts (30 to 40 feet) to test the speed of the green. Then hit some long breaking putts to test the amount the ball breaks on the green. Hit some medium-length putts from above, below, and on each side of the hole. Finally, hit a few short putts (two to three feet) in a row before you go to the tee. Don't worry if you don't make all of them; just maintain a good image of the ball falling into the hole.

Putting Rx: Remedies for Common Problems

Many players ask us the same questions about how to improve their putting. In this chapter, we present brief answers to the questions that players ask most often. Use this chapter for general reference to improve your putting. At the end of most sections is a guide directing you to the corresponding chapter(s) for supplemental information to read.

I can putt well on the practice green, but when I go on the course, I don't putt as well. This makes me doubt my putting ability. How can I putt as well on the course as I do in practice?

You diagnosed your own problem. The cause is doubt. You doubt your ability to putt well on the course and it becomes a self-fulfilling prophesy. You start to think you don't have putting ability and it becomes a reality. Here is what you can do to get back on track. First, change your thinking. You say you can putt well on the practice green, but then lose that ability once you get to the course. It's irrational to think you can putt on a practice green and walk a few feet onto a similar surface and feel you lose that ability. The physical components haven't changed. You play on a putting green no matter what you call it or label it.

The practice area is the same surface as the greens on the course. The only thing that changes is your attitude. It's the same task, but you turn it into a different animal when you step on the course. Think about all of the good strokes you have made when you were on the practice green. Pretend you are putting on a practice green. Remember the putts that you made. Replay those positive pictures of success in your mind and use the same stroke when you play on the course.

Secondly, you may be too score conscious. You won't putt your best if you focus on a score instead of your task. You place too much pressure on yourself to play for a score versus playing the game. Refer to Chapter 4, "The One-Putt Mindset: The Only Way to Think," and Chapter 5, "Confidence: The Key to Giving it Your Best Stroke."

When I see spike marks in my line, I get upset. I feel that I have no chance of making the putt. How should I handle this situation?

This is a common concern for many golfers. First, spike marks are inevitable. Golfers' spike marks are a part of the game. However, overreacting and becoming upset with spike marks doesn't allow you to put your best stroke on the ball. It causes more doubt about your line. Chances are, the putt may or may not be affected by the spike mark. It may even throw your ball back on line. You cannot control what happens to your ball once you hit it. Tour pros putt on greens that 150 other players trampled for five or six days of heavy play. The leaders make putts on greens that are heavily spiked. They know they have to putt through spike marks, but they don't let spike marks alter their strategy. You should do the same. Stay committed to your line and hit the putt squarely and firmly. A putt that is hit solidly will hold its line better. Don't allow a spike mark to fluster and distract you from your real mission. After you putt, tap down the spike mark for the next player. Someone may do the same for you.

When everyone in my group is making putts but me, it bothers me and affects my putting. How can I deal with this?

You let the actions of other people influence your putting. You are busy comparing your putting performance to everyone around you. You must focus on your game. No one else can play your game. Understand that if others are making putts, there is no logical reason that you shouldn't be making putts as well.

Instead of feeling bad because other players are holing their putts, find a way to feed off their good fortune as well. Great putting is contagious. Catch their fever.

You may start looking for excuses for not putting as well as others. Many golfers say that they have terrible luck and something interfered with their ball, and so on. The best thing to do is to stay focused on the things that you can control. The other members of your group are playing their game; you should be playing yours. The only difference is that they don't allow others' putting success, or lack of success, to interfere with what they are doing to be successful.

I think I'm a good putter. I make my share of par and bogey putts, but I don't make many birdie putts. Why is it that I can make par and bogey putts, but I can't make the same putts for birdies?

You label putts. You label the putt that you are trying to make as a "bogey," "par," or "birdie," which places limitations on your perform-ance. You may focus more intensely on some putts and not on others. A putt is a putt is a putt, no matter what you are putting for. The task is still the same—to hit a small round ball into a hole in the green. You need to dedicate the same focus and intention to every putt. You want to try to make everything, despite the putt's meaning.

For example, when a player hits the green in regulation he says, "I can two-putt and still make par." This is unproductive thinking. The player lacks the intensive focus needed to make putts. Every putt has the same probability of being made, whatever its label. How often do you notice that you were concentrating well on the par and bogey putts, but when you had a birdie or eagle putt, you just wanted to get it close? Do not handcuff yourself with this type of thinking. This causes you to become score conscious. Labeling can be devastating to the golfer who says, "I must make this putt to make my par." This will only produce anxiety and cause you to focus on the outcome. Remember that a putt is a putt and all putts can be made, despite how you label the putt.

Whenever everyone else in the group has made their putt and I am the last to putt, I have this feeling that someone has to miss. I feel it must be me. How can I change this attitude?

Ask yourself this question: Does the hole keep count of how many putts have or haven't been made in your putting group? The hole doesn't keep count or score; golfers do. This is a mental obstacle to putting. Players become so involved in the score, they forget the task is to find a way to get the ball into the hole. The remedy is to not concern yourself with everyone else's putt. Focus on what you need to do to make your putt. It shouldn't matter what anyone else has done on the putting green.

If everyone in your group is making putts, it makes sense to believe that the hole might be getting bigger for your putt. If everyone else can do it, so can you. It should give you a boost of confidence. There shouldn't be any logical reason to think that your ball can't go into the hole as well. Stay focused and make a good putt, whatever the outcome.

Whenever I'm putting well, I "see" the line very clearly. However, some days I don't see the line well. What can I do to see my line on those days?

Golfers who are putting well see their putting lines clearly. First, they can view their putting line on the green clearly and can run their eyes back and forth from the hole to the ball without losing their target. Second, a clear picture of the line helps players sense how hard they must hit the ball. When you have a good sense of speed and line, you will probably putt well. In essence, you have developed a strong visual and tactile sensation of where and how hard to hit the ball.

If you have a hard time seeing your line on the green, try the following suggestions. Be sure you are doing everything possible to read the green accurately. Closely inspect the putting surface and undulations to provide clues to see the line. Second, be specific with your target. Make a chain of spots that you link together to form a line. Linking the spots together into a long, continuous chain in your mind's eye gives you a stronger line impression than just looking at the ball and hole alone. Third, stay focused visually when you are moving into the putting position from behind the ball. Don't take your eyes off your line or spots. Watch your line as you approach to give you a stronger sense of where you want the ball to travel, even when your lines are cloudy. If these suggestions don't work, try picking an intermediate target and don't worry that you have not seen the line. Refer to Chapter 7, "Now You See It: Vision and Imagination in Putting."

How can I overcome the "Yips"?

The "yips" are one of golf's most perplexing dilemmas. Golf is no fun if you suffer from the yips. The yips have driven more good golfers to ruin than any other golfing illness. Fully eliminating the yips takes time and discipline, but there is hope. First, when a player thinks he has the yips, he has labeled himself as a sick putter. When a person loses all putting confidence, the fear of putting takes over. This is different from the simple fear of missing. Players who suffer the fear of putting just don't want to putt. The more they putt, the worse it gets, until it's intolerable. This leads golfers to believe they have an affliction. Whenever golfers condition themselves into accepting and believing something, it is extremely hard for change to occur.

What you need to do is take action. Build yourself a fluid and simple routine. Be sure about your line and strategy. Simplify your method. Step into your putt with only one focus: to contact the ball squarely. Track your target line by moving your eyes up and down the target line. Be ready to pull the trigger as your eyes return to the ball. This helps your body and eyes stay in continual motion. A visual shift acts as a trigger mechanism, much like a forward press in the putting stroke. Continuous motion prevents you from freezing over the ball. If you can keep your mind actively processing information, you will have a much better chance of stroking the putt without a muscle spasm, and forcing the putter back and through. You are replacing fear and frozen inactivity with positive mental action. It doesn't matter if your routine has a countdown procedure or a visual shift element. The key is to have a systematic routine that allows you to stay in control when fear is present.

What is the best way to practice before I go to the course when I don't have much time to warm up? How can I develop touch quickly?

A good method of practice, especially if you don't have much time to warm up, is mental practice. When you drive to the course, think about making good putts. You can replay putts you made in recent rounds or tournaments. Rehearse how the ball rolled over and over and toppled into the hole. Imagine the good feelings that you experienced. Let those feelings provide you with a sense of putting confidence and relaxation. Also, see yourself being successful with difficult putts under pressure situations. This gives you a sense of deja vu when you play. You always want to visualize yourself playing and putting well on the course you are about to play. This type of mental practice is highly effective for golfers as well as other professional athletes. See yourself putting with complete self-control. Imagine being totally self-confident when you stride up to the green. Imagine yourself stroking the ball toward the cup and bending down to pull it out of the cup. You can even visualize your fellow golfers saying, "Congratulations, good putt."

If you only have a little time to warm up, you may just want to stroke five or six balls back and forth on the green from a desired distance and focus on hitting them solidly. This will give you feedback that should help you negotiate distance and have touch on the opening holes. End your session by holing a few short putts. This gives you confidence to make crucial three-footers on the opening holes. It also helps to create a mental set of positive pictures. Most important, you should feel mentally and physically ready to play and have confidence you can make your first few putts. Refer to Chapter 10, "Preparing Yourself to Putt Your Best."

When I play with poor putters, they get me down. They are so negative. They talk about how they can't buy a putt. I try to not let them bother me, but sometimes I can't help it. How can I not let other players affect me?

You are letting others affect your mind and mood. If you listen to enough negativism, you become negative unless you learn how to stay in your own cocoon of concentration. Choose to focus on your game rather than the words of others. If you study poor putters, you'll notice that they talk themselves into a poor putting day. They miss one and then complain about the greens, the ball, the noise, or whatever. Something is always holding them back from having a good putting day. They do not realize that their negative self-talk reinforces their negative outcomes. You cannot control how others act and react to their own putting, but you can control your actions. You can choose to listen to their negativism and let it affect you. Or, you can choose to tune them out and stay focused on your game, and reinforce what you are doing well. Stay committed to your putting routine and strategy and do your best to not watch, listen, or buy into what the negative sellers are marketing.

The greens that I putt on are really smooth. When I go to other courses, the greens aren't as smooth as the one I play on and I think I won't putt well. How can I putt well on greens that are lousy?

It sounds like you putt on greens that are in superb condition. If you play many different courses, you should realize that not all greens are equal. If you have trouble adapting to poor greens, here are some suggestions. First, develop a mindset that allows you to be flexible. If you are going to putt on greens that are bumpy, hairy, or inconsistent, you have to learn to love whatever conditions you will putt on that day. Golf course greens are inflexible, and cannot change their present condition. But you can change and be flexible. You have the power to choose to accept the greens in their present condition and adjust to them, or you can complain, become negative and frustrate yourself. Choose to be a productive thinker.

If you have to putt on greens that resemble peanut brittle, you need to say to yourself, "I can putt well on peanut brittle." If the greens are super-slick, you need to remind yourself you are a great fast-green putter and slick greens roll the ball great. Conversely, if you are going to putt on slow greens, you need to remind yourself you love to putt on slow greens and can be super aggressive. This attitude helps you be flexible and overcome whatever difficulty you may encounter on less than perfect greens.

Second, use practice time to help develop your feel and touch on unfamiliar greens. Spend a little more time in your pre-round warm up, judging the pace and texture of the practice green. On the course, look closely at the green for subtle clues that help you develop your putting strategy. You may want to closely watch other members of your group putt. This will give you extra clues about the speed, texture, break, and other indicators that could help you putt.

Third, resist the temptation to speak or even think negatively about the playing conditions of the course. Speaking negatively about the greens is an excuse golfers use for their own inability to adapt to difficult conditions. Most important, whatever putting surface you play on, stay focused on the things that you can control.

It's hard to putt through my shadow. It is unnerving to me because I can't get my line correctly. I get a little nervous because I don't know exactly what's going to happen. What should I do?

The first thing to do is be sure about your line. As you set-up to the ball, make sure that you pick a spot that is separate from your line. This spot should be a target point for where you want the ball to go. It can be at the beginning or end of your putt, somewhere outside of the shadowed area. The shadow may interfere with your ability to see the line, and this is what is most bothersome. Your line distorts when you move your eyes up and down the line. This is unsettling, but can be overcome. Pick a spot or mark and putt freely without hesitation or doubt. If you watch your shadow instead of maintaining focus on the ball or contact point, you will not hit the putt solidly. Maintain your focus on your spot and hit a solid putt.

I know I have a sound stroke, but I seem to miss short putts. I make my share of long and middle-distance putts. However, I become nervous on putts of three feet or less. Why can't I make as many short putts?

You suffer from labeling your putts or identifying a length at which you become nervous. You can handle a 10- to 15-foot putt because you're not expected to make them all. Not unlike millions of golfers, the closer you get to the hole, the more anxious you become. You say, "Don't miss this one again." Or, "Oh no, here's another miss coming up." Sound familiar?

Second, you feel less pressure to make longer putts than shorter ones because of your expectations. Most players expect to make the shorter putts, but don't expect to make the longer ones. This pressures you into making the short putts. This increases anxiety and makes short putts more difficult than they really are. Missing short putt after short putt makes one feel incompetent. Lack of competence erodes your self-confidence.

You are suffering from a condition known as "musterbation." Musterbation describes a feeling players have that says "I must make this putt," or "I should make this putt." What usually happens is players tense up and become nervous and get in their own way.

First, if you have a sound putting stroke, you can make putts. Second, make sure you take the same time to read the green before you address the putt. Third, don't deviate from your normal routine. Stay focused on stroking the ball solidly on the line you want it to travel. Finally, understand that once you contact the ball, there is nothing more that you can do. The fate of the outcome is out of your control at this point. Live with the results and move on. Also, you may want to practice more short putts during warm up before you go out to play. Doing this will help reinforce success pictures in your putting memory bank.

When I'm over my putt, sometimes I get distracted and know I'm not ready, but I don't stop. I have heard that when you back away, it is sure death for missing the putt. What should I do when this happens?

If you are over the putt and feel you're not ready to putt, it is a sure sign you're not focused. Knowing you are not ready, but refusing to back away, doesn't allow you to putt the ball with total confidence. Self-doubt and indecision are the primary reasons for missing putts. It just doesn't make any sense when you know you aren't ready to go ahead and putt. You have to be 100 percent committed to the ingredients of your routine and sinking the putt. If you are not focused on execution, you are not ready to hit the putt. It's that simple. Make sure you are into the task before you putt.

Secondly, you say you've heard that backing away increases your chances of missing. When players feel they are not ready, we feel it is best to back away. This is a sign that you are not concentrating. You need to refocus. Step away and start your routine over. This allows you the time to refocus and be ready when it is time to putt.

In the 1978 U.S. Open at Cherry Hills Golf Club, Andy North needed a four-foot bogey putt to claim victory on the last hole over rivals J.C. Snead and Dave Stockton. When Andy got over the putt, a gust of wind came up and knocked him slightly off balance. Instead of battling the wind and hitting it anyway, Andy backed off. Hushed moans were heard throughout the crowd. The crowd thought it was inevitable that he would miss. However, Andy regrouped and went through his preputt routine for a second time. Again, when he was about to putt, something distracted him and he backed away again. After brushing himself off and refocusing, he set-up over the ball for the third time. He pulled the trigger back and stroked the ball into the heart of the cup to seal his victory and walk away with a U.S. Open Championship. The point is, if you know you aren't ready, you should back away, refocus your mind, and go through your entire routine. Give 100 percent mental commitment to being ready to stroke the ball into the hole.

On some days I don't have the feel I need to putt well. Something doesn't feel right. What can I do to regain my sense of feel on the greens?

You will have days when you don't have good touch on the greens, especially if you are a "feel" player. We can think of many reasons for losing your feel on the green. You may miss some putts early and start to doubt your ability. Your set-up feels wrong and this doesn't let you feel comfortable over the ball. You can't see the line like you usually do.

When you lose the feel, try adjusting the basics in your putting. First, try loosening your grip on the putter, or perhaps taking your glove off. Check your alignment and aim. Check your ball position. Look at your address position. Are your eyes over the ball on your putting line? Sometimes making a small adjustment can make you feel more relaxed over the ball, and relaxation means confidence. Don't assume you are not going to putt well that day, or that you've lost your feel for the day. Check the basics and stick with your normal routine. Remember to stay patient and roll the ball as well as you can.

A Summary of Great Putting: Six Important Keys

Now you know that to be a good putter, you must have more than a good putting stroke. A consistent stroke is just a part of being a good putter. No one has the perfect method for stroking a putt. Besides, golf is a game of scoring, not a stroking game. After you ingrain a stroke, great putting involves confidence, trust, and the ability to repeat that stroke. The better your attitude, the more putts you make. If you are just beginning to play golf, forming a repeatable stroke and developing your mental skills are equally important. If you are a low-handicap player, who already has a solid stroke, developing mental skills and improving your attitude should be given top priority.

We discussed several topics on the psychology of great putting—from developing confidence to improving your focus. We reiterate several themes throughout the book to reinforce what we think are the most important mental keys to great putting. These keys are: attitude, confidence, touch and feel, total focus, imagination, and trust. The following sections summarize the keys to using your mind to putt your best. You should devote most of your energy to improving these six areas. Also, after you finish reading *The Mental Art of Putting*, review the six keys monthly using this chapter.

POSITIVE ATTITUDE

A positive attitude allows you to approach each putt with full intention and focus. Your attitude should help you believe in your ability and putt the ball where you have programmed yourself to hit it, without doubt. This is the true key to using your mind to putt your best. A positive attitude also implies seeing yourself as a great putter, knowing you can improve, filling yourself with positive feelings and emotions, and trusting your judgement on the green. A good attitude is essential regardless of the number of putts you have made or missed. Developing a positive attitude should be your starting point to great putting. Great putting begins with attitude. Don't wait until you have that first good putting day to believe in your putting ability.

PUTTING CONFIDENCE

Building and preserving your confidence is a central theme discussed throughout the book. This should take top priority in your training program. You can't be a great putter without total self-confidence. You might have a great stoke, but its worthless without the confidence to back it up. Confidence means believing that you can make putts, but it is more than this. Confidence comes from thinking you are a good putter, developing competence in your skills on the green, relying on quality practice, and not letting a bad putting day ruin your belief.

Developing and maintaining confidence is an unending project. We have no quick fixes when it comes to developing real confidence. But we do know that you should focus on what you can control and not waste energy worrying about what you can't control. You control your attitude, confidence level, and practice, and how you react to lipping-out. You can't change the fact that you lipped-out a three-footer, but you can choose how you react to that situation. This is the central theme of *The Mental Art of Putting*—having the power to choose your attitude and react to events with optimism and purpose.

Let's face it, there will be times when the strength of your confidence is tested. Missing short putts, three-putting, and not making anything can pull you down, but only if you let it. Confidence can weaken because of poor self-talk or other ways in which you negatively view situations. If you are critical, judgmental, or self-degrading, your confidence must suffer. Criticizing yourself is

> ## Great putting is a combination of several key human components.
>
> - **Confidence**
> - **Imagination**
> - **Touch/Feel**
> - **Attitude**
>
> - **Belief in Self**
> - **Total Focus**
> - **Trust**

very harmful to your self-confidence. Remember to monitor your self-talk and make every effort to use positive self-talk. Take responsibility today and think, act, and feel as if you are a good putter.

TOUCH AND FEEL

All great putters talk about the importance of touch in putting. There are two important elements in putting: starting your ball on line, and hitting your ball with the correct speed. Most three-putts result from hitting the ball too long or too short of the cup. Therefore, the ability to gauge and control your speed is crucial to your putting success. On breaking putts, the line you select also is dictated by the velocity of your ball. Given the same putt, you need to play more break with a putt that is hit softer, and play less break with a putt that is hit firmer. Thus, touch is important for judging and regulating speed and for estimating how a ball will break given its velocity.

As stated earlier, touch is the ability to gauge your distance from a target and hit your putt with the right speed. Feel is the kinesthetic feedback you receive that helps develop your sense of touch. Touch comes from experience and practice. If you have never hit a 20-foot putt, you have no memory of what it feels like to hit a 20-footer. But as you practice, you learn to judge how hard to hit that 20-foot putt. The better your touch, the more confident you are that you can roll the ball with the correct speed.

Improving your touch should be a priority for developing confidence. We discussed a few exercises for improving your touch on the greens in Chapter 11.

You can take those drills a step further and invent your own drills. The goal is to create as many different experiences as possible by hitting putts from different distances and with different breaks. Your touch will not improve if you only practice straight 10-foot putts. Varying your practice distances helps you transfer your practice to the course.

TOTAL FOCUS

Most golfers have adequate powers of concentration when no distractions are present. But problems start when players face fear, anxiety, pressure, and external distractions. In Chapter 6, we discussed the six elements of good concentration. These include: (1) knowing what cues on which to focus; (2) staying focused on those cues; (3) keeping a narrow and external focus; (4) shifting attention when needed; (5) knowing how to refocus when distracted; and (6) controlling your thoughts.

If you want to improve your concentration, we give some exercises in Chapter 6 to practice off the course. But ultimately, when you play, you must train yourself to focus on the cues that are important to your performance and disregard irrelevant cues or things that you cannot control.

The two most important keys to concentrating well on the course are: (1) stay in the present and think one shot at a time, and (2) focus on the ingredients of your routine. Most errors of concentration come from thinking ahead about the results and consequences of a shot, or from thinking about the last shot you just hit into the trees. If you can play one shot at a time, you won't get ahead of yourself and think results. Also, when you focus on your routine and the steps that help you hit a good putt, you are focused on the present moment and on the task.

IMAGINATION AND VISION

The mind and body follow the input from the eyes. Golf is a visual game, and putting is a highly visual task. Putting is similar to playing darts; it's a target game. If you can't see the bullseye, you can't aim at the target. Your vision and imagination are crucial to successful putting. You read a putt by predicting and seeing how your ball will react on the green, which requires imagination. Your eyes also guide your alignment and aim.

In Chapter 7, we discuss how to use your vision to gain visual cues to read putts accurately and how your eyes can be used as a trigger for your stroke. Using your eyes to putt well boils down to training yourself to see the cues that help you perform, and programming yourself with your mind's eye. You must interpret several pieces of information to read how your ball reacts on the green. Then you must make an educated decision (or educated guess if you're unsure) about what the ball will do.

As you approach the ball, your eyes should be target-fixated. At this point, we could debate whether your eyes should focus on the hole, a spot near the hole, or an intermediate spot on your line. But we recommend looking at a specific spot near or in the hole and using a soft focus to engage with the line. If the line fades, you still have the spot on your line on which to focus.

What should you look at when you stroke the ball: the ball, the hole, or your putter? First, we strongly discourage you from looking at your putter as you stroke the ball. This causes you to control your putter head. Most players watch the ball during the stroke, but also retain the ball-target orientation and/or sight their line with peripheral vision.

TRUSTING YOUR STROKE

Another important key to using your mind to putt your best is the ability to trust your stroke. Some players can trust their stroke better than others. Trusting your stroke is the opposite of relying on mechanics to stroke the putt. You practice to ingrain a reliable stroke. You don't want to practice your stroke when you play golf. This is the time to let your creative mind hit the ball. If you can hit the ball solidly with your eyes closed, you can trust your stroke in a match. Trust is the mental glue that bonds the components of great putting together.

Now is the time to get target-oriented. At the most, you should focus on the tempo of your stroke or the feel of solid contact. Don't get wrapped up in how to get the ball to the hole. Shift your focus to seeing your line, focusing on the ball, and launching the ball to the target. Get into feeling the ball to the hole.

MONITORING YOUR PROGRESS

Now you have the keys to great putting. Improving your mental skills requires a continued effort. If your attitude is not up to par, don't expect an overnight cure. No one can give you a positive attitude but yourself. You must go with the flow when you're putting well, but you must know how to mentally adjust when struggling. Stick to your philosophy and don't cash in the chips if you don't hit the jackpot on your first try.

Discipline is a do-it-yourself project. Now it's up to you to apply what you have learned about great putting to your own game. This book will help you get started, but it's your choice to finish the job. Begin to apply the information and make it work for you. To help monitor your progress, we have provided a Player Progress Questionnaire in the Appendix. Make some photocopies of the questionnaire or buy a notebook in which to write. Answer the questions after each round and evaluate your progress. Remember to use your mind to putt your best!

Player Progress Questionnaire

Tournament _____ **Date** _____

1. Describe your putting confidence for this round. How did you improve or maintain your confidence? What hurt it?

2. How was your attitude about putting this day? How did you deal with negative thoughts and negative self-talk?

3. What did you do to be totally focused on every putt? How will you improve your concentration for the next round?

4. How often (what percent) did you do your routine for putts? When did your routine break down and how did it break down?

5. How well did you read the greens? When you couldn't "see" your-putting line, what did you do?

6. How strong was your trust today? Did you become mechanical with your stroke at any time? If so, when?

7. What did you learn that will be helpful for the next round or tournament?

8. Rate your putting: (Poor)1   2   3   4   5   6   7   8   9   10(Great)

9. What else would you like to note about your putting?

References

Brown, H.J. (1991). *Life's Little Instruction Book*. Rutledge Hill Press: Nashville, TN.

Cohn, P.J., & Winters, R. (1995). *The Psychology of Putting: Perspective from Tour Pros*. Peak Performance Sports: Naples, FL.

Graham, D. (1990). *Mental Toughness Training for Golf*. Steven Green-Pellham Books: New York, NY.

Green, H. (1994). *Think 1-2 on Every Shot*. In Swing Thoughts (Don Wade, Ed.). Contemporary Books: Chicago, IL.

Hanson, T. (1992). *The Mental Aspects of Hitting*. Unpublished Doctoral Dissertation, University of Virginia: Charlottesville, VA.

Hemery, D. (1986). *Sporting Excellence: A Study of Sport's Highest Achievers*. Human Kinetics: Champaign, IL.

Hogan, B. (1957). *Five lessons: The modern fundamentals of golf*. Simon & Schuster: New York, NY.

John-Roger, & McWilliams, P. (1989). *You Can't Afford the Luxury of a Negative Thought*. Prelude Press: Los Angeles, CA.

Kite, T. & Dennis, L. (1990). *How to Play Consistent Golf*. Golf Digest/Tennis Inc.: Trumbull, CT.

Lopez, N., & Wade, D. (1987). *Nancy Lopez's The Compete Golfer*. Contemporary Books: Chicago, IL.

Nicklaus, J. & Bowden, K. (1974). *Golf My Way*. Simon & Schuster: New York, NY.

Norman, G., & Peper, G. (1988). *Shark Attack! Greg Norman's Guide to Aggressive Golf.* Simon & Schuster: New York, NY.

Palmer, A. & Dovereiner, P. (1986). *Arnold Palmer's Complete Book of Putting.* (p.24). Atheneum: New York, NY.

Pelz, D. (1989). *Putt Like the Pros.* Harper & Row: New York, NY.

Peper, G. (1988, December). *Profile: Gary Player Outspoken!* Golf Magazine (p. 26). Times-Mirror Magazines: New York, NY.

Rotella, R. (Speaker). (1986). *Putting Out of Your Mind.* (Cassette Recording). Golf Digest/Tennis Inc. New York Times Company: New York.

Strange, C. (1990). *Win and Win Again.* Contemporary Books: Chicago, IL.

Winters, R., & Cohn, P.J. (1995). *Collegiate Golf Coaches Philosophy and Psychology of Putting: A Case Study Approach.* Peak Performance Sports: Naples, FL.

About Patrick J. Cohn, Ph.D.

Dr. Patrick J. Cohn heads Peak Performance Sports. A leading sport and golf psychologist, author, and professional speaker, Dr. Cohn teaches his methods to golfers on the PGA Tour, LPGA Tour, Buy.com Tour, Golden Bear Tour, and several collegiate and amateur players. Dr. Cohn earned a Ph.D. in sport psychology from the University of Virginia in 1991. Experts in sports psychology consider him as the leading authority on preshot routines and putting psychology. Dr. Cohn's mental game programs were developed from more than a decade of work and research with world-class golfers. He is the author of *The Mental Game of Golf: A Guide to Peak Performance, Peak Performance Golf: How Good Golfers Become Great Ones, Going Low: How to Break Your Scoring Barrier,* and coauthor of *The Mental Art of Putting: Using Your Mind to Putt Your Best.* He stars in the audio book *Think to Win: How to Manage Your Mind on the Golf Course* and the video *Make Your Most Confident Stroke: A Guide to a One-Putt Mindset* and costars in the audio *Great Putting—Right Now! Mental Keys to Confident Putting.* Dr. Cohn offers sports psychology seminars to golf clubs, golf schools, athletic trainers, health care professionals, and business people and groups. The PGA of America approves his education seminars for education credits. He has appeared twice as a special guest on the Golf Channel. He is also a regular columnist for golfweb.com and his articles have appeared in *GOLF Magazine, PGA Magazine,* and *Golfweek.*

Contact Dr. Patrick Cohn at:
Peak Performance Sports
7380 Sand Lake Rd.
Suite 500, PBM 5012
Orlando, Florida 32819
Phone: 407-909-1700
Toll-free: 888-742-7225
E-mail: pcohn@peaksports
Website: www.peaksports.com

About Robert K. Winters, Ph.D., Sports Psychologist and Performance Consultant

Dr. Robert K. Winters is a sport psychologist from Orlando, Florida, and completed his Ph.D. in sports psychology at the University of Virginia. He also holds Bachelor of Science and Master of Arts degrees from Ball State University, where he played on the college golf team and served as a captain during his senior year. Dr. Winters was also a touring golf professional in the late 1970s and has attended the PGA Qualifying school as a participant.

Dr. Winters is the coauthor of the book *The Mental Art of Putting: Using Your Mind to Putt Your Best!* and the coauthor of two audiocassettes, *Great Putting—Right Now!* and *Golf Confidence for Women.* He is also the coauthor of a new CD entitled *Golf Confidence for Juniors.* Dr. Winters is a contributing writer for *Golf International Magazine, Michigan Golfer Magazine.* He is the director of NIKE Golf Schools at the Boca Raton Resort and Club in Boca Raton, Florida, and also the NIKE Golf Schools at Williams College in Williamstown, Massachusetts.

Dr. Winters is an advisory member of the National Association of Golf Coach Educators and is a member of the National Golf Foundation Association of Golf Educators, the American Counseling Association, and several national sport psychology and physical education organizations.

Dr. Winters consults with touring professionals on the PGA, Senior PGA, LPGA, and Buy.com golf tours and works with athletes of all levels and several men's and women's collegiate golf teams. He is a leading researcher in confidence and motivation, putting confidence and sports vision. He is the resident sport psychologist for the David Leadbetter Golf Academy at Champions Gate in Orlando and is the president of his own performance enhancement company, Mind Power Sports, located in Orlando, Florida.

To contact Dr. Winters, email him at mindpowersports@aol.com.

Peak Performance Sports
Mental Game of Golf Library

Books for Developing a Winning Mindset

Going Low: How to Break Your Individual Scoring Barrier by Thinking Like a Pro
Teaches tour-proven mental strategies for any golfer who wants to break his or her
individual scoring barrier—whether it's 100, 90, 80, or 70—and continue to shoot
low scores. Drawing heavily from the experience of top professionals' career low
rounds and his work, Dr. Patrick Cohn provides specific methods that will guide
golfers, lesson by lesson, toward their dreamed-about personal best round. Golfers
learn, for the first time, how to avoid expectations and overcome comfort zones in
golf. 170 pages, $22.95 U.S.

Peak Performance Golf: How Good Golfers Become Great Ones
For serious students of the game who want to improve their overall performance, this
unique guide teaches intermediate to better golfers how to get the most out of their
abilities, prepare their best for competition, and lower their scores. Dr. Cohn teaches
golfers how to develop a plan for practice, reach for their dreams, take care of one's
body, eat healthy foods for golf, improve physical fitness, prepare the mind for play,
and improve practice habits. 221 pages, $16.95 U.S.

The Mental Game of Golf: A Guide to Peak Performance
Written by Dr. Patrick J. Cohn, noted consultant to tour pros, *The Mental Game of Golf* teaches golfers how to master their mental game and play with greater confidence and composure. Learn how to find the zone more often. It combines the author's work, research, and tips from tour pros to illustrate the mental skills and routines needed to play your best. 169 pages, $16.95 U.S.

Other Resources for Developing a Winning Mindset

Great Putting—Right Now! Mental Keys to Confident Putting (audio)
Read by Dr. Patrick J. Cohn and Robert Winters, MA., two leading experts in putting psychology. Golfers learn to create a great putting attitude right away, putt with more confidence, and a fearless attitude. Learn how to putt and think like a great putter and use the power of choice to be more confident and focused. Perfect for golfers who are streaky putters or players who struggle with putting! 1 Audio Tape: 74 minutes, $12.00 U.S.

Think to Win: How to Manage Your Mind on the Golf Course (audio)
Read by Dr. Patrick J. Cohn, this two-tape audio program teaches golfers how to avoid self-sabotage and take their practice game to the course. This unique instruction program gives golfers field-tested practical strategies to help transfer their skills to the course, practice better, find the zone, and play with confidence, composure, and consistency. 2 audiotapes, 110 minutes, $18.95 U.S.

Make Your Most Confident Stroke: A Guide to a One-Putt Mindset (video)
Dr. Patrick J. Cohn along with PGA Tour player Grant Waite give you the secrets to being confident, focused, and free on the greens. They show you how to develop a confident putting routine so you can focus on the task and make more putts. Drills for developing touch to eliminate three putting are also included. 1 video, 37 minutes, $22.95 U.S.

Peak Performance Golf Insights (newsletter)
Dr. Cohn discusses how to apply specific sport psychology techniques to your golf game. Includes quotes from tour pros and the latest methods he uses in golf psychology. 2 issues (Spring and Fall), $10.00 U.S. per one-year subscription